AFRICAN
AMERICAN
CHURCH
GROWTH

AFRICAN AMERICAN CHURCH GROWTH

12 Principles of Prophetic Ministry

Carlyle Fielding Stewart

Abingdon Press
Nashville

AFRICAN AMERICAN CHURCH GROWTH:
12 PRINCIPLES OF PROPHETIC MINISTRY

Copyright © 1994 by Abingdon Press

This book is printed on recycled, acid-free paper.

Library of Congress Cataloging-in-Publication Data

Stewart, Carlyle Fielding, 1951–
    African American church growth:12 principles of prophetic ministry/Carlyle Fielding Stewart.
        p.   cm.
    Includes bibliographical references.
    ISBN 0-687-16541-5 (pbk.:alk. paper)
    1. Afro-American churches. 2. Church growth—United States.
I. Title.
BR563.N4S77   1993
253'.089'96073—dc20   93-5062

Scripture quotations are from the New Revised Standard Version Bible, Copyright 1989 by the Division of Christian Education of the National Council of the Churches of Christ in the USA. Used by permission.

94 95 96 97 98 99 00 01 02 03 — 10 9 8 7 6 5 4 3 2 1

MANUFACTURED IN THE UNITED STATES OF AMERICA

TO
Bishop Edsel A. Ammons, Dr. Anthony J. Shipley,
Dr. Donald A. Scavella, Dr. Hycel B. Taylor, the Reverend
Philemon Titus, the Reverend Robert G. Williams,
Paul Franklyn, and Henry Mitchell,
spiritual warriors of the faith,
who have stayed on the Lord's battlefield

AND TO

The people of Hope United Methodist Church,
Southfield, Michigan, for their love, support,
and faithful service in the Lord's work

If farmers do not cultivate their fields, the people in town will die of hunger.

AFRICAN PROVERB

Foreword

In *African American Church Growth,* Carlyle Fielding Stewart has provided a convincing and insightful formula for the healthy, responsible, and qualitative growth of all churches and other faith communities. He has broken fresh ground by providing for churches what Janice Hale, A. W. Boykin, and Asa Hilliard have provided in the field of education. The church and the academy must be adapted to the cultural context which they seek to serve.

Dr. Stewart is a rare breed of scholar who is also a powerful, dramatic, and persuasive preacher. In addition, he is a caring and compassionate pastor. Both his writing and his preaching are authenticated and enriched by intellectual discipline, pastoral experience, ethical conviction, and prophetic commitment. The world needs to hear from writers who are thoroughly acquainted with their subject matter. That is why *African American Church Growth* is "must" reading for clergy and laity of all colors, churches, and nations.

Though it specifically addresses the issue of effective ministry in partnership with the African American community, it is indicative of the understanding and sensitivity that make preaching and teaching effective in other ethnic and cultural milieux. Those who would teach, preach, or sell among Asians, Hispanics, Africans, or Southern Europeans may learn from Dr. Stewart to become conversant in their languages, values, concerns, and challenges. We must not arrogantly impose our culture upon others, but must learn alternative ways and forms in which the substance of our faith may be richly and effectively shared.

Those who happen to be specifically interested in planting and growing churches in the dark ghettos of urban America or in the integrated neighborhoods of suburban existence will be greatly benefited by Dr. Stewart's excellent research, analysis, and directives. Having wonderfully developed and strengthened Hope United Methodist Church in Southfield, Michigan, Dr. Stewart has demonstrated that a church in transition need not be a church in decline, and that diverse cultural and racial modes of worship and service need not compete, but may complement each other harmoniously, so that the subtleties, complexities, and nuances of the human spirit may be skillfully addressed.

Celebrated black preachers in predominantly white churches have learned to create wholistic styles of ministry which utilize the best traditions of two cultures that had been alienated by bigotry and irrational fear. Yet despite the existence of racial myths and psycho-socioeconomic barriers, there is something in whites that craves the dynamism and vitality of the African American soul. The Beatles, Elvis Presley, and New Kids on the Block have earned international fame and fortune by using African American musical forms, rhythms, inflections, and emotional improvisations. Qualitative African American preachers recognize, likewise, that there is something in the souls of African Americans that responds positively to organizational structure, intellectual content, and the planned order of European culture.

European Americans and African Americans have helped to create each other. We are simultaneously baroque and impressionistic, classical and modern, European and African. Therefore, the white preacher who is compulsively mechanical, wooden, and structured will fail to attract, excite, or sustain many white worshipers. Likewise, the black preacher who is wildly emotional and disordered will be too chaotic and esoteric to attract and hold the growing black middle class, which has adopted enough Eurocentric teaching and experience to look for some aspects of them in their language, music, business, and worship.

We make haste to commend Dr. Stewart for drawing no arbitrary line of infinite qualitative distinction between African and European cultures. A glance at the Egyptian pyramids reveals that African culture is not totally spontaneous. Likewise, an evening of Italian grand opera is enough evidence that emotionalism is not a stranger to European experience. The challenge to both African Americans and European Americans is to learn enough from each other to get in touch with the essence of what it means to be human. In the deepest depths of human nature, all cultures converge to inspire and enrich one another. It is when we get in deepest touch with ourselves that we find ourselves in fullest partnership and fellowship with others.

Like Dr. Jeremiah A. Wright, Jr., senior minister of Trinity United Church of Christ in Chicago, Dr. Stewart is an excellent representative of a new generation of successful preachers who have "come to themselves" and are found to be intellectually sound, culturally sensitive, prophetically committed, and spiritually anointed. They will surely bring in the New Age of the American Church, because they have learned, in order to teach others, that people are people who need the bread of intellectual content and will respond to it if it is not presented in a cold and dry form. More important, they know that people must have spiritual vitality and will not reject it if and when it is made available to them in a form that is intellectually elucidating. Dr. Stewart is a great teacher, preacher, author, and pastor because he embodies the best of two worlds. Gleaning from the rich harvest of his mind and ministry is a profitable and beautiful engagement.

Charles G. Adams, Pastor
Hartford Memorial Baptist Church;
President, Progressive National Baptist
Convention, Inc.

Contents

Preface

Historically, the African American church has undergone several transformations. But in spite of these transformations, it has remained constant as a place of rest and protest for the well-being of African American people. Without its presence, the people would not have been able to rise from slavery and other forms of powerlessness.

This marvelous institution of learning, guidance, and insight is God-intended, God-inspired, and God-directed. It is indeed a precious gift of abundant good for the wholeness of African American people who find their way to its sanctuary.

The insights offered in this well-documented and most timely book lend themselves to enabling African American pastors to come to grips with the praxis of ministry, the principles that must be employed for effective ministry with African American people.

The message that emerges from the soul of the author is that there is an identifiable set of principles upon which the actions of ministry must rest and that this ministry must be reflective of the ethos and life of the African American experience. According to the author, and I unqualifiably agree, the primary objective of the prophetic church is the transformation, liberation, and personal empowerment of African American people.

I invite those who are in the tradition of the African American church movement, especially those interested in prophetic church growth, to enter into dialogue with the author to learn about prophetic growth for the African American church. In this dialogue, you will embark upon a journey that will equip you to lead your church in addressing the undefined and unanticipated challenges that the twenty-first century will bring.

In gratitude, I salute Carlyle Fielding Stewart for producing this teaching tool for ministry with African American people. I am overwhelmed by his forward look toward the future of the African American church.

Donald A. Scavella
Executive Secretary,
United Methodist Union
of Greater Detroit

Introduction

> *The task of prophetic ministry is to bring the claims of the tradition and situation of enculturation into effective interface.*
>
> Walter Bruggemann

> *Consciously or unconsciously, all African culture is deeply religious and celebrative, as well as involved in the material concerns of human existence.*
>
> Henry Mitchell

This book is written primarily for anyone interested in increasing the growth of a church by utilizing prophetic principles, but more specifically, it addresses black churches in mainstream predominantly white Protestant denominations. Traditionally, such churches have had difficulty in reaching large segments of the African American community because the styles of worship and cultural assumptions for carrying out ministry have appealed more to the values of their European counterparts than to the African American masses. While a number of such denominations boast of having respectable numbers of African American members within their ranks, these figures pale in comparison to those denominations whose models of ministry are more ostensibly charismatic, Afrocentric, and prophetic.

A central thesis of this book is that black churches can build viable congregations within mainstream denominations by employing principles of church growth which reflect a prophetic concern for the ethos and life of the African American experience. Such emphases have always been a hallmark of strong black churches.

Historically speaking, the African American church has always had a prophetic role in black life in America. From the beginning of the slave experience to the present moment, black preachers and congregations have played a vital part in articulating issues related to social justice, the eradication of racism and poverty, and they have called the "powers and principalities" into account over the enslavement and mistreatment of African American people.

Moreover, prophetic concern has not simply taken the form of public pronouncements against the evils of slavery, racism, and other social and spiritual maladies, but is equally manifested in passionate witness to God's salvific and liberating grace within the context of human history and the beloved community. Thus the form, content, and trajectory of prophetic principles, as expressed through the mission and ministry of the Afrocentric church, have invariably personified a unique spirit whose gifts include unbridled passion and enthusiasm for the Lord's work.

Of all the texts recently written on church growth, few have seriously explored how prophetic principles can be usefully employed to establish vital congregations. Many strategies include the development of marketing techniques to lure baby boomers. Other books propose overhauling denominational structures to promote organizational and evangelical effectiveness within the local church. Statistical data have disclosed and confirmed the mathematical formulas of church growth and decline. The roles of pastors and laity in growing churches have been debated, evaluated, and debated again. Despite these worthy efforts, the prophetic-relational components of church growth have not been addressed.

If prophetic ministry has proved to be a successful tool in developing black churches, why haven't more churches utilized this model? What are prophetic principles for church growth, and how does one implement them to build vital congregations?

This book offers some ideas on increasing black church membership prophetically. Based on ten years' experience in building a strong black church in a predominantly white denomination, it seeks to help any pastor or lay person interested in revitalizing a local congregation. These precepts are presented as simply and concisely as possible and should facilitate the development of a model of ministry which embraces the unique aspects of the African American experience.

For our purposes, the primary goal of the prophetic church is to call the people back to God. We must, by developing ministries and programs which increase spiritual awareness, take the lead in promoting personal and social transformation. The primary objective of the prophetic church is the transformation, liberation, and personal empowerment of African American people, so that they might actualize their optimum potential and realize human wholeness. The prophetic model of ministry requires positive change through constructive action in all aspects of African American life.

CHAPTER ONE

Four Tenets
of Prophetic Engagement

Ministry based on prophetic principles can help urban black pastors develop viable black congregations. But in order to increase membership, black urban churches, in particular, must develop a mission and ministry which speak to the vital concerns of the communities they serve. What are the attributes and biblical foundations of prophetic ministry, and how might these tenets enhance our understanding of ministry to African American communities?

The word *prophetic* tends to evoke images of peace, personal and communal wholeness, and social justice. The prophets Amos, Jeremiah, and Isaiah clearly personify the Old Testament model of prophets who stand before the powers and principalities—the kingdoms and rulers of this world—calling them into account with the words, "Thus saith the Lord." The concern for social justice, as embodied within the life of the covenant community, is an important element in understanding the mission and ministry of the Old Testament prophets.

Walter Brueggemann delineates the importance of the prophet in serving as both *criticizer* of the existing order and *energizer* of persons and communities, moving them back to the central issues of their faith—those which, by providing an alternative consciousness toward the world, supply the community of believers with a new vitality and understanding of their own wholeness and possibilities.[1]

While concern for social justice is traditionally perceived to be the primary goal of prophetic ministry, a more important issue is the need to energetically call people back to the central claims of their faith, and to witness to them in ways which encourage full ownership and participation in that revitalization process. As both criticizer of the established order and energizer of God's people, the prophet calls attention to the importance of covenantal responsibility and commitment in the formation of vital communities. Such exhortation is compelled by the need for an alternative consciousness, a radical transformative awareness which reveals the what, when, and how of God's saving and liberating acts within human history. The efficacy of the prophetic office is thus embodied in the *content* and *form* of the prophetic message. The success of prophetic ministry is not determined solely by the *words* of the message, but by the exigency and urgency with which those words are conveyed to the people of God.

For our purposes, prophetic ministry is defined as: *The process of calling the people of God into an awareness of God's saving, liberating and redemptive acts so as to compel the radical participation of individuals and communities in spiritual, social and personal transformation. The result of that transformation will be the realization of human wholeness and potential in the present, as well as in the future.*

Such ministry is indispensable to community development and revitalization, and thus is an essential element in the prophetic growth of African-American churches.

Four basic tenets serve as presuppositions to prophetic ministry and dynamic church growth and have Old and New Testament foundations: *passion-compassion, conviction, investment,* and *vision.*

PROPHETIC PASSION

The Old Testament presents the image of prophets as people of *passion* and *compassion.* The dynamic energy with which they went about their tasks is indispensable to the external demands placed upon them by the prophetic office. The ability to feel, to sense viscerally the Word of God, and to respond with *heart, head,* and *soul* in the context of community, is critical to prophetic church growth.

Passion is the fuel which empowers the messenger to bring forth the Word of God. This Word, powerfully moving across the lips of the messenger, must be thought and felt. A fervor, a desire to tell and to be told, to witness to the dynamic, energizing, and transforming Word of God, is felt by the messenger and by those to whom he or she is sent. Whether in Jeremiah's weeping and lament or Isaiah's fierce diatribes against the nation of Judah, we see that this prophetic passion—the ability to sense, interpret, and soulfully articulate God's Word—is an important dimension of prophetic life and ministry.

A young minister pastoring a Presbyterian church in a large predominantly black community in Chicago lamented that few blacks attended his church. He decried that other more charismatic churches in the community were filled to capacity on Sunday morning, while his was virtually empty.[2] He later discovered that both the image of Presbyterianism in the minds of black people and the style of worship his church presented to visitors discouraged growth. His worship services lacked the vitality, conviction, and ardor which both invite and precipitate an increase in membership. No passion! No people!

Equally problematic was the congregation's lack of evangelical zeal in doing ministry in that community. If anything contributed to the decline in membership, it was the lack of prophetic passion in both preacher and parishioners.

The church attained a reputation for being dead, cold, without the energizing, revitalizing passion indispensable to growing churches. Such passion is also an important dynamic in African American culture and always has been a part of the expressive ethos of black life in America. *Those churches which exemplify passion in telling the story, preaching the word, and reaching out to others in the larger community have been most successful in building viable congregations.*

The Word of God teems with life. The church should be a creative life center, a dynamic force in the lives of God's people. Nothing stifles the church like lifelessness. Nothing dampens the spirit like listlessness and lack of enthusiasm.

In speaking of prophetic passion as a foundation for ministry, I am not referring to premeditated, orchestrated, untrammeled emotion. Too often, passion is identified as raw unchecked emotion. Emotion is an element of passion, but not always synonymous with it. White people often label the expressions of black sentiment as "emotional." Often they are. Black worship services are viewed by some whites as emotional outbursts, anguished outcries of primitive impulses. This viewpoint is shaped through cultural conditioning.

Thomas Kochman says that a primary difference between Afrocentric and Eurocentric forms of cultural expression is the level of passion or feeling used to communicate ideas.[3] In black culture, passion is often indispensable to personal expression, even when it borders on the emotional. In white culture, passion and emotion often interfere with rational processes and are generally negated as viable forms of communication. Emotion, for whites, disrupts rational reasoning. Emotion, for blacks, helps to convey the importance of reason.

To show passion in ministry is to exemplify the vital dynamic and energizing forces which come from hearing, knowing, feeling, and sharing the Word of God. A preacher may deliver a passionate sermon without being emotional, but seldom delivers an emotional sermon without some passion. The desire to express oneself passionately is similar to what the prophet Jeremiah spoke of as "fire shut in my bones." This expression of feeling has always been a distinguishing characteristic of African American culture and a benchmark of black church worship.

One factor that contributes to the positive success in membership growth of blacks in the more charismatic denominations has been the ability to *let the spirit flow.* Letting the spirit have its way really is an expression of freedom, and this always has been central to the tradition and norms of the African American religious experience.

Put in language different from that of the charismatic world, a key to prophetic ministry is the cultivation of a *vocabulary of caring,* a vocabulary that is vitally connected to the critical issues of those to whom such love is given. In order to care, one must have passion, or compassion, for those to whom one is sent. This passion is expressed as genuine concern for the well-being and wholeness of others individually, as they realize their unique gifts and graces under God, and collectively, as they share the claims of their faith within the larger community.

The prophet is a messenger who brings the Word of God to the people of God, but the act of proclamation is always issued out of a passionate concern for the life, health, and ultimate vitality of God's people. Social justice and political freedom cannot be realized unless there first is one who cares enough to issue the claims passionately and publicly. The public pronouncements must be rooted in a genuine love for God's people. And this passion must be conveyed through the mission and ministry of the church.

Too frequently, black ministers who serve predominantly white denominations alienate large segments of the black community in their effort to emulate Euro-American styles of ministry. The absence of feeling in worship, evangelism, preaching, teaching, and in relating to the ultimate concerns of the black life is a key factor in that estrangement. One Episcopalian minister virtually bragged about how successfully his church reflected the cultural norms and attitudes of whites in his denomination. "Emotionalism is not tolerated in our church. My people don't want that! It violates their sensibilities." In talking further with him, he revealed that this attitude reflects a behavioral norm of the white Anglican tradition.[4]

Expected to not demonstrate emotion in sermon delivery or identify with the behavioral norms of African American culture, any indication of spontaneous passion meant the manifestation of sentiments which impeded ministerial objectivity. This perspective, primarily Eurocentric, often retards the growth of black churches in predominantly urban black environments, because passion and emotion are important aspects of black life and symbolize the aliveness, vitality, and freedom which constitute human wholeness and religious precocity. Blacks often identify the absence of passion as being synonymous with white norms and values. If feeling is not expressed in the context of church life, blacks generally will not see it as an authentically black church and thereby may choose not to join it.

The trouble with this view is that it uncritically reflects the consciousness and mores of the white Episcopalian status quo. The presuppositions for doing ministry are not rooted in the folkways, traditions, and mores of African American life and culture. Meanwhile, the church is surrounded by a community that is alive, pulsating with music, crying, laughter, passionate expressions of the rhythms and polyrhythms of African American culture and life. Without a passion genuinely rooted in that culture, churches that follow the norms and values of the Euro-American culture exclusively will largely not realize their optimum growth potential. *If one is to make a black church grow prophetically in a black community, one must identify with the culture of African American people and implement aspects of that culture in the life of the church.*

The words of Amos, Jeremiah, and Isaiah reveal a dimension of human concern and empathy for the people of God that is unpretentious. Amos says, "Let justice roll down like waters, and righteousness like an everflowing stream" (5:24). Jeremiah declares, "A voice on the bare heights is heard, the plaintive weeping of Israel's children, because they have perverted their way, they have forgotten the LORD their God" (3:21). Isaiah exhorts, "Draw near, O nations, to hear; O peoples, give heed! Let the earth hear, and all that fills it; the world, and all that comes from it!" (34:1). Even in the life of Jesus we find the words: "When he saw the crowds, he had *compassion* for them, because they were harassed and helpless, like sheep without a shepherd" (Matt. 9:36, italics added).

The passion of the biblical prophets did much to convince the people of God of the sincerity and efficacy of God's Word during their time. Imagine the pronouncements of Isaiah without the zestful appeal to the human heart and conscience, or the utterances of Jeremiah spoken without the convicting sentiments which moved even him to tears.

Passion exhorts and convinces hearers of the imperatives of constructive action. How shall the prophets convince their hearers unless they too are compelled by the fervency and urgency of the message? How are preachers and laity to build viable churches without the passion which moves human hearts and challenges human minds? Something must exist in the mission and ministry of the church which arrests and convinces, which captivates and rejuvenates those who live among the "tombs" of this world. Something must reside in the life of the church that reaches out to people with the honesty, sincerity, and integrity which only human sentiment can personify.

The prophets were successful in their ministries partly because of their ability to convince the people of God that God truly cared about them and that their positive response to God's Word could make a qualitative difference in their individual lives and in the collective covenant community. The ability to convince the children of God and inspire them to responsible action was based in part upon the deeper human connections which resulted from the prophet's message, and also upon the community of caring and concern which responded to that message. It was precisely in the creation of the nurturing, caring community in response to the prophet's word that Israel and other prophetically inspired communities were able to attain their peculiar status.

The same fervency and sincerity embodied in the prophet's message is needed today in building viable churches. Ministers and laity must personify a similar concern as they exhort people to return to God. Passion and compassion cut through the deception and duplicity of the world and create a context for the genuine, mutual, transformative discovery of God's Word in human community.

Amid life-threatening chaos and the whirlwinds and meaninglessness of the present epoch, passionate and compassionate people seek the recovery of lost souls and the restoration of meaning and purpose for God's people. The church grounded in prophetic ministry can do much to win souls to Christ by demonstrating a genuine zeal in its service to the people of God and to those who need but have not yet found God.

PROPHETIC CONVICTION

Passion and compassion are the first marks of biblical prophecy and prophetic church growth, but *prophetic conviction* marks the second tenet. Conviction is simply the irrepressible desire or will to "live the Word" through human experience. It is the persuasion that empowers human action and is strongly based upon faith and belief. Passion without conviction is like an engine without oil or a car without fuel. I recently observed a placard on a colleague's office door, attributed to a book by Josh McDowell (*Evidence Which Demands a Verdict*): "If you were on trial for being a Christian, would there be enough evidence to *convict* you?" Conviction measures the length and breadth of the believer's desire to demonstrate the central tenets of faith and belief. How far are you willing to go to convince people of the meaning of God's Word? Would you be willing to die for your convictions as Jesus died? A statement which might be called a conviction is the famous axiom of Dietrich Bonhoeffer: "When Christ calls a man, he bids him come and die."[5]

Convictions are intimately bound to beliefs, which are tied to the feelings and passions that influence human behavior. The pastor's convictions are important elements in building viable ministry, for they often speak of commitment to Christ and his ministry. The adage, "If a person won't stand for something, he'll fall for anything," reflects the importance of conviction. How convicted or convinced are we of the power and import of God we serve? How far will we go to win persons to Christ?

Where the secular overshadows the sacred, where cultural and religious norms seem shaped more by the larger society than by the church and religion appears locked in a fierce struggle with the world for the souls of God's people, religious belief and conviction can become passports into people's hearts.

The prophets of the Old Testament believed so strongly in the efficacy of the prophetic office and God's Word, that they were willing to be convicted for their beliefs! And many of them were actually executed. The same conviction unto death was shown by Jesus, Paul, the apostles, and many believers of the early church. A similar capacity and courage are needed today for pastors seeking to build and expand churches in the urban black communities, where hopelessness, despair, and poverty threaten to snuff out the lives of God's people. Pastors must stand for the truth and the promises of the gospel. This is the cross all of us must bear: We must stand for love and truth amid the hatred, untruth, and apostasy of the world.

A pastor in Ohio, serving a church of 150 people, once made a disturbing comment which runs contrary to prophetic conviction: "I never do or say anything that will rile my parishioners. Life's too short for that. I have to take care of my family, provide for their needs. If I make people angry by what I say, I lessen my opportunity to eat."[6]

Conviction also involves *courage*, the ability to take stands that may be unpopular with parishioners, but may ultimately lead them to a new awareness of God's creative, transformative possibilities in their lives and in their communities. This involves a level of *risk taking*—"placing the hide on the line," in the words of my late grandfather—which means not taking a Faustian bow to amenities and trappings of the world, but standing true and tried in its assemblies. Henry David Thoreau, in response to criticism of his dogged determination and conviction, said that even one on the side of God constitutes a majority.

The possession of prophetic conviction does not mean that pastors only lead crusades for social justice, but that they equally demonstrate conviction and faith in dealing with the tyrannies of parish life. Dissension and strife often destroy churches. But while exerting prophetic conviction, pastors must not ascribe to themselves undue arrogation of power. When demonstrating prophetic concern, pastors must become part of the solution, not part of the problem.

A pastor of a United Methodist church in Michigan conveyed frustration in dealing with and ministering to three families who had controlled the church for twenty years. He related the following story:

> For the first three years of my ministry, I failed to address an issue I knew was killing the morale and spirit of parishioners of the church. Three or four families had always dictated policy to the ministers who came to serve there. Their power was never challenged by other families in the church, and many of the people who joined under my leadership left in frustration. Fearing reprisals and retaliation from the Pastor-Parish Relations Committee, and these few families, I remained silent and failed to witness to the convictions which had initially drawn me to the ministry. I literally abandoned any convictions I had about right, truth, and justice, in order to get along with these people.[7]

The tragedy of this scenario is that, due to a failure in prophetic conviction, that church never achieved its growth potential. Without oversimplifying, a failure of faith on the part of the clergy and lay leadership often sounds the death knell for potentially viable congregations. In not taking a stand that by conviction he was perfectly right in taking, he became a "co-conspirator" of the havoc which eventually wrecked his church. Albert Einstein once observed, paraphrasing a statement by Edmund Burke, "The only way for evil to prevail is for the good to remain silent." By remaining silent, a pastor chooses the path of least resistance, and the church often pays a heavy price.

What essentially occurred through the "rulership" of those few families in that church, was a consolidation of political power, which poses a far greater tyranny in a church's life than the threat of any external political power. The upshot of a failure in prophetic conviction on the part of the clergy and laity in that church was an unwarranted, unjustified ecclesial death. Unquickened resolve and the reluctance to take a firm prophetic stand against such forces precipitated the demise of a potentially viable congregation.

Prophetic ministry thus means addressing concerns and issues in the larger social arena, but equally witnessing to those forces, powers, and principalities which stifle the church from within, thus thwarting the full emergence of the redemptive community.

Pastors should be willing to present and embody an alternative consciousness, to stand on the convictions of love, truth, and justice in fulfilling the high calling of the ministerial office. Having courage to take a stand for right means risking something on behalf of God; be willing to redemptively suffer the possibilities of ostracism, ridicule, even annihilation, by not allowing evil to overrun and destroy the church. Conceding to evil persons who rule and subjugate the church, who undermine its mission through power politics and the insidious manipulation of church polity for personal ends and gains, is a failure to come to terms prophetically with the essence and meaning of personal conviction in leading the people of God to build the kingdom of God.

Chogyam Trungpa, in his work *Shambhala*, delineates the warrior principle of spiritual leadership.[8] Pastors are sacred warriors, called by God to be courageous in the leadership of God's people. The apostle Paul speaks of "putting on the full armor of God"

(Eph. 6:11). Trungpa says that sacred warriors do not wage war in the tradition of Valhalla. Unlike conventional warriors or those called mercenaries, violence is not their forte. *They are warriors because of the absence of fear and the presence of a confidence or conviction which makes them intrepid in owning and being what they truly are. They are motivated by an ultimate concern for the well-being and wholeness of the people they serve. In essence, they are ambassadors of goodness.*

Prophetic ministry stands on the same surety of conviction. Here we do not mean that the pastor should become a self-righteous purveyor of religious precepts or a Grand Inquisitor, impulsively castigating and punishing people for their imperfections. Rather, pastors are called to stand firm and tall against the forces of evil, corruption, and injustice, both in and outside the church. The same zeal with which they stand against the tyrannies of church life also should compel pastors to place themselves on trial for the wrongs and injustices they may have committed in the execution of the office of ministry.[9] In the challenge to address these major concerns, pastors can easily become agents of abuse, called to pronounce judgment in the name of God, but exempting themselves from that judgment in leading the people of God.

Thus a humble willingness to take a position of moral agency in the ebb and flow of parish relations is an important element of prophetic ministry. Walter Brueggemann is again helpful here:

> The task of prophetic ministry is to nurture, nourish, and evoke a consciousness and perception alternative to the consciousness and perception of the dominant culture. Thus I suggest that prophetic ministry has to do not primarily with addressing specific public crisis but with addressing in season, the dominant crisis that is enduring and resilient of having our vocation co-opted and domesticated.[10]

The process of being domesticated or co-opted can easily occur in parish life when the health and vitality of a church are based upon allegiances formed around the establishment of cooperative relationships. In volunteer organizations such as the church, pastors can ill afford to give up their prophetic "birthright" in exchange for personal loyalties. They must not be afraid to speak their minds and challenge people to do what's good, right, and just. But their moral authority is augmented by their ability to follow the prescripts they offer to parishioners. Their conviction must be buttressed by a willingness to live morally and ethically within the parameters of God's word.

The prophetic conviction exemplified by the biblical prophets was strengthened also by the urgency of their pronouncements. There is no failure of nerve on the part of the prophet, no second thoughts about the levity and legitimacy of the message. The messenger is utterly convicted and convinced by the truth of God's revelation, and must tell others!

How far did the prophets go to convey this message? As stated earlier, many gave their lives, were imprisoned, tortured, and executed for their beliefs. Their convictions were so strong, their faith so undaunted, that they dared speak to both rulers and ruled, nations and individuals, about the impending judgment of God. And so it is in parish life. Prophetic ministry requires both the conviction and assurance that the Word, as it is preached and lived, is God's very own. Without prophetic conviction, the willingness to take risks and be risked on behalf of God's beloved community, the pastor cannot adequately convince others of the credence and truth of God's Word. While many of the people did not heed the voice of the prophets, few could dispute the sincerity of their proclamations and the conviction with which the Word of God was spoken.

As ministers of the gospel, how far are we willing to go to serve God's people? Would we, like Jesus and the former prophets, be willing to give our lives because we believe so deeply in the truth of God's Word? Or do we lack the conviction, the gall, the nerve to dare speak in accordance with the revelation we have received?

In an age of doubt, duplicity, half-truths, cynicism, despair, and outright disbelief, the prophetic church must speak directly and pointedly to the issues of our times if it is to win the minds and hearts of God's people. Do the messengers themselves believe so strongly in that message that its principles and truths are manifested in their lives? What are the depths of their convictions, and to what breadth and length will they go to win people to God, to convince them of the gospel's imperatives, and to challenge those who do not see the light to catch sight of the Kingdom and all of its glory?

Prophetic conviction is a sine qua non for building the church prophetically, and it has strong biblical precedents in the experience of Jesus and the prophets of Israel.

PROPHETIC INVESTMENT

Another important gift exemplified by the biblical prophets and helpful to those developing prophetic ministries is personal *investment*. Not only are passion and conviction hallmarks of a prophetic pastorate, but a desire to fully and unequivocally invest oneself in serving the Lord is necessary.

The problem of investment on the part of clergy in the parishes and communities they serve is particularly acute in itinerant systems such as that of The United Methodist Church. Here short-term pastorates are more the rule than the exception, and many pastors, when called to serve, find it difficult to fully invest themselves or cast their nets where they are sent. Not that these clergy are indolent or apathetic, but the frequency of movement gives rise to transient expectations which make a full investment of oneself in the long-term growth of a church virtually impossible.

In the experience of Jonah, the temptation to avoid personal investment in the enterprise of God was very troublesome. Jonah knew the dangers of going to Nineveh and wanted no part of it. The price for such personal investment was too high, and Jonah took a boat to Tarshish instead. Personal investment often means paying with one's life, and for some, this is too much to ask.

Moses and Jeremiah probably were reluctant to lead God's people because they had counted the cost of service. Moses excused himself because of a speech impediment, and Jeremiah used his youth as a disclaimer.

Whatever one's rationale, the reality of personal investment cannot be circumvented if one is trying to build a church by using prophetic principles.

Investment also can be viewed from a New Testament vantage point. Is not the incarnation God's investment of himself in the person of Jesus? "God so loved the world that he gave his only begotten son." This is the ultimate investment in humanity—placing one's very own life on the line to save and liberate humankind.

Incarnation means personal investment; a *kenosis,* or emptying of oneself, into service to God's people. Here no holds are barred, no excuses for service and work are given. The lines are drawn, and one chooses to either invest or disinvest in the mission and ministry of the church. A colleague related the following experience:

> When I first moved to my new appointment, I went out into the community as I had always done in the initial stages of my pastorates. There I introduced myself to people in the community and talked with them on the street. One day I met a man and introduced myself as the pastor of St. James Church. I shall never forget the curious look he gave me. Then came these words: "This is the first time I've ever come face to face with a minister of your church. I've lived in this neighborhood for over forty years and have never been able to get the church involved in the life of the community. The pastors never returned my calls and seemed uninterested in this community."[11]

This is a clear indication of how a church can have a profile of disinterest or disinvestment in the life of a community. That church simply had a poor image. It had detached itself from the mainstream of community life. As the neighborhood increased in lower-middle-income people, the church failed to invite them in or place itself on the cutting edge of community concerns. By divesting itself of the life of the community, it obviated any chances for vital growth.

Prophetic ministry is the ministry of investment, of relating to people around critical issues of their lives. As one wag stated, "It's not your ability but your availability that counts in this profession." That church, by divesting itself of the life of the community, conveyed an image of unconcern.

Without the proper investment of time, care, and resources available to those in the surrounding community, it is plausible that a church will achieve only nominal, if any, growth.

The life of the larger covenant community was always of central concern to the biblical prophets. They all seem to have shared a common goal in restoring Israel's relationship with God. Having a stake in its success and future, they wholly put themselves into the task of bringing to reality the will of God. This meant the proper investment of time and energy so that the beloved community could experience wholeness by realizing its optimum gifts and potential. Thus investment must be preceded by a genuine giving of self, resources, and time, which are indispensable for church growth.

The principle of prophetic investment calls to mind the necessity of preparation, contemplation, and evaluation of the ministry and mission of the church. The greatest investment is time, because it's the only thing you can give others and never get back. Time is indispensable in ministry. Without the investment of time and a desire to work faithfully and diligently for the Lord, goals and objectives for church growth cannot be realized.

In reading the prophets, it is clear that a great investment of time went into the preparation of their messages. Even those proclamations which arose spontaneously in the glint of a moment were preceded by an investment of time and an outpouring of the self in the preparation process. Prophetic investment is the ability to place oneself wholly, and without reservation or impediment, in the preparation of a ministry which will ultimately bring persons to Christ. Any church seeking to grow prophetically must seriously consider the importance and necessity of prophetic investment.

PROPHETIC VISION

The fourth and final characteristic of prophetic ministry is *vision*. With *passion and compassion* for God's people, a willingness to stand on justice and truth through firm *convictions*, coupled with an *investment of self*, comes the honing of the prophetic vision.

The prophetic church is one that dares to ask, "Where would God have us go? What must we do to get there?" Vision is a necessary part of prophetic ministry, for the pastor as prophet must have an eye for the future, taking people and moving them toward the higher reality.

The challenge of Moses' ministry was not merely a geographical or topographical relocation of God's people, but equally, the movement of their minds, hearts, and spirits into an alternative consciousness of their value and worth as a liberated people.

Some have termed this "kingdom consciousness"—the aware-ness of God's presence in all endeavors, and the shaping of human belief and action based upon such awareness. The prophetic utter-ances of Isaiah and Daniel were inspired by a glorious vision of the dawning of a new age, when God would forever reign and the full personhood of their people would finally be restored.

One writer states that the prophet was not so much a predictor of events as a harbinger of calling people back to God. A vision of the future required the cultivation of insight and foresight which heralded God's future plan for the people. The prophets had a vision. Edgar Magnin makes the following observation: "Isaiah envisioned the day when the lion would lie down with the lamb; when swords would be turned into plowshares . . . when every man would dwell under his own vine and fig tree and none would be afraid."[12]

Precisely because virtually all other agencies in society had been institutionalized or co-opted, the prophet's value lay in the ability to stand outside and call them into account. This calling was informed in part by a *vision* of the possibilities of human transformation within the context of a corrupt social order. Thus the social order itself could experience renewal and transforma-tion through the dynamic alteration of the human personalities who administered the institutions.

Prophetic vision is especially critical as a catalyst in African American communities. Perhaps no other segment of American society is so intimately aware of the imperatives of social and personal transformation.

A *vision* of an ideal America sparked the emergence of the Civil Rights and Black Power movements. "Liberty and justice for all" is a cry rooted in the American dream, a dream based upon a vision of equality, justice, and prosperity for all people.

The church that takes a prophetic stand on issues vital to the life of African American communities, and then voices its con-cerns in the public and private arenas, is generally motivated by a concern for justice, prompted by a vision of peace. This vision is rooted in a hope and faith that God's will can and shall prevail in the context of human community. It wasn't until one pastor began to openly address some developers' insidious displacement of community residents that his church experienced membership growth. He made the following observation:

> I guess people want to see the church and ministers take a stand on issues critical to their needs, rather than hiding behind the collar. It wasn't until the church took a firm stand on the issues—and the developers were clearly motivated by nothing but greed—that the church began to grow.[13]

For some, this correlation of church growth and community involvement may seem tenuous. But for African American people, the church is still the most vitally progressive force in the life of their communities. If the church remains silent in the midst of the evils of injustice, how will the people have a voice to adjudicate their concerns? This particular church experienced growth because community residents knew it was concerned about the rights of its citizens. Whenever a church speaks out with righteous indignation, its stature often rises in the eyes of the community.

In further discussions with this pastor, I discovered that his initial motivation for becoming involved was based not only upon a genuine concern for his people, but upon a *vision* of a better community. This image was inspired by a prophetic notion of the church as a catalyst and herald of positive spiritual and social change in the lives of community residents. Before entering the crucible of social justice, this pastor had developed a reputation among his parishioners for playing fair and being unafraid to speak the truth.

It was not enough for the Old Testament prophet to simply have a vision of the new heaven and earth. He must have been empowered by what he saw, even when few others saw it, and he possessed the courage to actualize the vision in real life. Ministry today is often stifled by preoccupation with immediacy, and pastors are stymied by an inability to make their vision reality. One reason mainline Protestant denominations have lost potential black members may have been their failure to maintain vigilance against racism and the other forms of social and communal injustice that are not part of the larger vision of the kingdom of God.

The possession of prophetic vision also means anticipation of the future and preparation for it in the present. Ezekiel's visions *anticipated* the cataclysmic events in the lives of his people. Nehemiah awaited a return to Jerusalem to rebuild the wall, even amid threats to his life and peer rebuke. Amos understood the imperatives for social justice and clearly saw them prefigured on the very land where he tended his flocks.

The prophetic dimensions of Jesus' mission and ministry were based upon visions of a new heaven and a new earth. His entire focus was on building the kingdom of God in the here and now, and preparing people for its coming. It is essential to have an understanding of what life can be, in order to bring the vision into reality.

The ability to *anticipate,* to *expect,* to *envision,* and to *implement* God's vision for the people is a critical component of prophetic ministry and a useful aid in promoting church growth.

These four principles of prophetic ministry, rooted in the biblical understanding of prophecy, are indispensable elements in cultivating the prophetic church. They are equally important in understanding both the text and the context of African American life and culture. Without *passion, conviction, investment,* and *vision,* black churches, particularly in predominantly white Protestant denominations, will seldom realize their potential.

CHAPTER TWO

Prophetic Attributes of Ministry

The Positive Norms of African American Culture

Increasing the growth of black churches through the use of prophetic principles requires an understanding of black culture and needs. It is difficult to increase church membership without grasping those principles which motivate black people to join churches. The principles are very different from those in Euro-American white churches.

An appreciation and respect for the nuances and particularities of black culture is especially important to blacks who serve in predominantly white denominations. Pastors in these churches should be aware of the needs of the congregations and communities they serve, because these denominations tend to have low profiles in African American communities. For example, overall, there are more black Baptists, Apostolics, and Pentecostals than black United Methodists, Presbyterians, Episcopalians, or Lutherans. The latter denominations, which are largely white and Eurocentric, have appealed less to blacks in general than those in which the style of church polity and mode of worship are more consistent with the presuppositions of black culture.

To dramatically increase membership, it is necessary to understand and value the positive norms of African American culture. The following delineation of such norms is based upon the spiritual, psychological, and cultural needs of black people. These norms are by no means exhaustive, but are useful starting points for understanding the context of African American church growth.

VALUING THE TRUTH OF ONE'S EXISTENCE

Any serious undertaking of black church growth must first consider the importance of Afrocentric values. What are the rhythms, sounds, textures, colors, expectations, and assumptions of the black experience as it is lived within the context of American life? "Walking the walk and talking the talk" of black life is a primary expression of Afrocentricity.

The first norm, *valuing the truth of one's existence as a primary mode of being and acting in the world,* is philosophically known as the legitimation of one's beingness. It is also defined as black self-esteem, in psychological terms. Being truthful about oneself is to recognize the positive and negative aspects of black life. One must be unafraid to be oneself, to own and express the existential and ontological truth of one's being and existence in the world. Being authentic, or true to "the grain of one's wood," is a most important ingredient in understanding the dynamics of black culture in America.

Too often, black pastors who serve white denominations and desire to emulate their *white peers* will negate their Afrocentricity in an appeal to white cultural norms and values. Such attitudes are often translated into worship services that are sedate and tranquil, without the customary dynamism and enthusiasm emblematic of black culture. Sermons often lack the verve and verse of prophetic persuasion, or are simply without the passion or conviction which inspires black audiences.

In white denominations in general, black clergy observe an apparent devaluation, contempt, or suspicion of any ethos that authentically resembles the rhythms, forms, and expressions of black life and culture. I shall never forget an experience I had preaching to a predominantly white audience in a suburban church. The theme of the conference was "Celebrating the Black Experience" and it addressed concerns around racism in the church. After preaching the sermon in the customary enthusiastic black-church style, a white clergyman approached me unsolicited and proceeded to criticize my mode of delivery. "Your content was fine. It was the *way* you delivered the sermon, that I didn't like." He was accustomed to hearing sermons delivered in the conventional conversational monotone that many white preachers have adopted. Such styles are largely consistent with Euro-American culture. Any show of enthusiasm or emotion in the pulpit is synonymous with losing control of oneself. In black culture, such expression means "letting the Spirit flow." We were separated by our perceptions about what was appropriate sermon delivery. Such perceptions are often conditioned by race and culture.

The problem here is not that worship forms or ecclesial styles can be multifaceted, which should prompt the celebration of the diversity of white and black cultures. The trouble is the devaluation of Afrocentricity as a viable expression of an authentic experience of God. Nothing is more troublesome than white or black brethren denigrating black culture as a viable, authentic, reasonable, and worthy context in which to do ministry and build churches. Nothing is more reprehensible than black people apologizing to white people for black culture or culturally nuanced styles of ministry.

Such strict adherence to the formal tenets of a denomination, or what has evolved into a "white style," runs counter to the evangelical principles as well as the dynamics of religious freedom espoused by the prophetic African American church. This formal restriction to a white Eurocentric style by blacks has done much to prevent the growth of the African American church in predominantly white denominations.

Black people, by and large, do not join churches because they are Presbyterian, Episcopalian, or United Methodist—that is to say, for name only. When these denominations are mentioned, one invariably conceptualizes a specific style of worship, preaching, or governance which characterizes the church's image of outreach to the community. It is generally the *style* of these denominations which does not appeal to the black masses.

As a rule, blacks largely identify or unite with specific congregations because the church meets some deeper spiritual need or speaks fervently to those issues of "ultimate concern" which affect the individual. Subsequently, they choose a particular denomination because it meets some ontological need and has some functional value in helping them cope with life in all its grandeur and terror.

The ideal church embraces a mosaic of individuals and cultural expressions. There is a diligent effort on the part of some whites to understand, appreciate, and celebrate the cultural traditions of the black church. However, because mainline Protestant denominations remain predominantly white institutions, the authentic black church often becomes a white church with a black face, because both blacks and whites often devalue the authenticity of black culture as a meaningful context of authentic religious experience.

Without oversimplifying, it is safe to say that black culture has a particular style, feel, rhythm, and ethos different from that of white culture. This is not a put-down of Eurocentric forms of church life. Black culture constitutes a specific trajectory of being which includes unique ways of knowing, seeing, feeling, interpreting, responding to, and shaping the world around it.

Being truthful about and valuing the truth of one's existence means recognizing and owning both the positive and the negative attributes of one's culture and life.

The pastor serving a black congregation in the inner city would do well to be in touch with the norms and forms of African American culture. He or she must be unafraid to be authentically black; to "walk the walk" and "talk the talk" of African American people, if he or she expects to touch people in ways that will win them to Christ.

Jesus' speaking in parables was his way of walking the walk and talking the talk of the people of his time. In order to increase his disciples, he had to be familiar with the sights, sounds, nuances, and feeling tones of the people and culture to which he related. In other words, he had to know the culture and speak the language of the people so as to reach and move them.

The prophetic aspects of this endeavor are manifested in the willingness to be honest about the nature of one's being and existence, to shed the layers of pretense which inevitably shroud blacks who live in a white society. The prophets of old, always stripping themselves ontologically bare, unpretentiously stood before God and the community of believers, and owned in every way who and what they were. They did not negate their identities in order to appease the existing political powers.

Many black people expect their leaders to be comfortable with who and what they are, as the called and created of God. Owning one's identity is important in living authentically, and living authentically is a critical aspect of black church growth. For to be true to what and who one is, as the created of God, encourages others to be authentically what and who they are. In paraphrasing a statement of John Oliver Killens, "Black people are the only people set aside because of their color and told by those who set them aside to forget their color."

Again, we see in Scripture the need to be stripped bare otologically and rationally. Jacob can no longer run from the truth of his existence and his transgression of Esau's birthright. He must come face to face with himself, own what he truly is, and come to terms with himself and God.

All the major and minor prophets had points of reckoning— times to shed the pretense and folly of their existence and stand truthfully before God. They had to come clean and true to God before being consecrated for the Lord's work.

The call and response pattern is very important in black culture, in part because of the need to express oneself openly and without the traditional constraints imposed by white society. Expressing oneself openly and honestly, or "telling it like it is," has virtually always meant certain death for black men in American society, particularly in the South. Many pathologies have developed from our inability to express the truth. The repression of authentic expression has invariably been the result of people daring to share the truth of their existence.

Thus being and telling the truth fulfills the need for self-expression and personal empowerment psychologically, and the black church is the arena in which that truth is spoken, actualized, interpreted, and fulfilled in a collective sense.

The African American pastor who would be prophetic must lay claim to the psychic truth of his or her own heritage and existence, and emphasize those realities essential to the psychological liberation and spiritual and personal transformation of African American people.

Living and being the truth of who and what one is, is not only psychologically empowering but spiritually liberating. If psychological truth serves as a basis for personal empowerment through the freedom of expression, spiritual truth contains elements of transcendence which catapult the believers beyond the constraints of their material condition. For example, when slaves were told by their masters that they were less than human and undeserving of the fullness of God's created order, spiritual truth allowed them to transcend the limitations of those conditions by envisioning themselves otherwise. Spiritual truth brought to their dire existence an element of transcendence, a "going beyond" the existential claims of their captors.

A black cultural norm consistent in prophetically increasing growth in the African American church is to own and claim the psychic and spiritual truth of one's existence, to value and celebrate the norms and nuances of truth in the African American tradition and heritage. This means not apologizing to white or black people for the existential truth of one's existence, an existence created authentically by God as a realization of full personhood.

DEVELOPING POSITIVE RELATIONSHIPS

The next important norm in African American culture, a useful strategy for increasing growth in churches, is *relational*. The relational aspects of black life and culture are essential in building community and sharing material and human resources.

How people get along by *relating* to one another is critical to solidifying diverse elements in the black community. Nowhere are these relationships more reinforced and dramatized than in the black church, which is a forum for the interpretation of the community's ongoing life. These relational principles also make sense outside the black culture, but the emphasis and nuances are obviously different.

Relational norms of black culture include the following: Valuing and respecting others as persons; developing relationships of mutual concern and trust; caring for and responding to the needs of the family, extended family, and community; raising and caring for elders, children, and adults; respecting the eminent domain of matriarchal and patriarchal authority; reverence for God and those spiritual sources which confer value upon human life.

The same relational principles that lead to strong families and communities are the building blocks of the African American church. Hospitality for those living within and outside the community is also essential to the community's relational life and is a vital element in church growth.

These relational norms work, because feeling, touching, seeing, and embracing—all are hallmarks of African American culture.

> A family strength, like the support network or system in which it operates, is any process or network of interactions that aids or helps individuals in anticipating, addressing, interpreting, managing and otherwise successfully responding to their concrete condition or situation.[1]

African American churches that are experiencing the greatest growth have established strong congregations through the development of meaningful interpersonal relationships created by a sense of family, which is the primary context for creating within the individual a sense of belonging. Developing relationships of mutual trust, respect, and harmony are essential to personal well-being, and personal well-being is critical to the development of strong communities.

In talking with numerous pastors throughout the country who have increased growth in black churches, I find that a common ingredient of their success is the emphasis on strong interpersonal relationships, which is the basis of viable ministry—the development of positive, relational norms which encourage respect, reciprocity, and the development of relational "cooperatives," which strengthen the larger community.

Caring for others, creating a sense of belonging through fellowship, building character and community through the mutual development of positive relationships—these are the norms of black culture essential to the growth of black churches.

When asked why she didn't join a certain church after a month of regular attendance, an elderly woman stated, "It just didn't *feel* right! I got the sense that people in the church were more interested in competing with each other than creating a sense of belonging—for the people who were there."[2]

Do the people who attend your church have a sense of belonging? Do they feel needed and wanted in the life of the congregation? Do the interpersonal relationships reflect caring and mutual trust? The church, along with the black family, remains the primary dispenser of care in African American communities. No other institution has as much influence in shaping the lives and values, and in creating a context for belonging, personal identity, and empowerment.

In an African American congregation, there are no strangers and all are welcomed into the household of God. This has always been a mainstay of black culture: the creation of hospitality and sense of belonging, where no outsiders exist. The same norm should be an integral part of the prophetic black church and, if established within the ethos of a church, will facilitate an invitation to others to be part of it.

The prophetic task in the larger community around the church is to invariably raise an awareness of the covenantal mandates that pertain when people belong to God. As the people of God relegate themselves to the status of outsiders through their own sin, the prophet calls them into awareness and the recognition of the imperatives of belonging which are established through the covenant. Those who have fallen outside must accept the challenge to come inside and experience the full covenantal benefit of God's grace and blessings.

The people of God are essentially the family of God, and successful ministry in black communities is closely tied to these familial norms and values, espoused mainly as prophetic principles. Mutual caring, trust, and respect are thus essential to this process.

Following are some critical questions relative to adopting and reinforcing positive black cultural norms in the prophetic church: To what extent does our church create a sense of hospitality and belonging for all who visit here? Do the interpersonal relationships and spirit of the congregation create an atmosphere of openness to which insiders and outsiders will choose to belong? Do we value the feelings and opinions of others as an essential aspect of community building, personal affirmation, and Christian growth? To what extent is a sense of family created by the fellowship and interaction of people within the church?

The emphasis must always be on creating a sense of openness, establishing hospitality, and developing a sense of family through networks of caring which evoke a desire for belonging. The feeling of belonging strengthens, uplifts, rejuvenates, and ultimately creates a context for a greater awareness of the self and its potential, which leads to personal empowerment and transformation.

A hallmark of Trinity United Church of Christ in Chicago, Illinois, and of Hartford Memorial Baptist Church in Detroit, Michigan, two of the fastest growing black churches in urban black America, is their emphasis on developing a black cultural context which speaks to the needs of urban blacks. Precepts of the Christian faith and the norms of black culture are combined to form both the context and the spiritual framework for ministry in the city. Pastors Jeremiah Wright and Charles Adams have developed programs and ministries which speak to issues of personal empowerment and transformation without violating the norms of Christian faith.

Their efforts have been duplicated by many other churches throughout the country. Second Baptist Church in Evanston, Illinois, and Ben Hill United Methodist Church in Atlanta, Georgia, along with others, have adopted similar styles of ministry.

Dr. Hycel Taylor at Second Baptist Church in Evanston has always emphasized the importance of the black church having a prophetic role in the confirmation and transformation of African American life and culture. He was one of the first to conceptualize and develop the prophetic model of ministry which has influenced my own development.

Again, the four dimensions of prophetic life are useful here, for without *passion, conviction, investment,* and *vision,* the church stands little chance of creating the context of belonging so indispensable to establishing those black cultural norms essential to prophetic black church growth.

IMPROVISATION, SPONTANEITY, INNOVATION

Much ministry in black communities is based upon the freedom to improvise, to be spontaneously led by the Holy Spirit, and as a result, to innovate new and creative models of ministry.

Improvisation, spontaneity, and innovation are closely tied to *adaptive and expressive needs.*[3] Numerous black churches in predominantly white denominations have tried to build churches according to the text of Euro-American experience. A need exists to follow the "book," but a need to not follow it when circumstances present is also a reality. The cultural, psychic, and spiritual elements that draw whites to churches may not attract blacks. While our psychic, spiritual, and material needs are similar, the patterns and symbols of acculturation and symbiosis are often different. Many of these churches have failed to grow because they do not accommodate the desire for improvisation, spontaneity, and innovation synonymous with certain aspects of the black experience.

This norm is closely tied to the *spirit-centered* methodology of African American churches. The Holy Spirit is an entity unto itself and one must be open to it at all times. The Spirit cannot be textualized, so to speak. It comes in its own time, works in its own way, and brings to fruition its own results. Openness to spontaneity and improvisation are essential to allow the Spirit to work in worship as well as in the overall life of the church.

This does not mean that spontaneity obviates a need for order, rationality, and planning. But with spontaneity comes a certain freedom to act in accordance with the ebb and flow of the Spirit. Such freedom cannot always be sequestered by order.

This also does not suggest that the textual approach to ministry should be abandoned for the sake of the Spirit. It simply means that, along with the text, there should be an openness to be led by the Spirit which may not be confined to every letter of the text. Both text and context, following the letter as well as the spirit of the law, are equally important.

I recall in my own personal experience the struggle between text and context, between following the letter of the law and the spirit of the law. Some denominational leaders firmly believed that ministerial methodologies at Hope United Methodist Church ran counter to the textual principles of The United Methodist Church. My style of ministry relied upon the *Discipline,* but also upon common sense. Reading the text and being led by the Spirit had always been twin constructs in my African American upbringing. Had I taken the suggestions of both white and black colleagues as to the best way to increase growth in Hope Church, the church would have foundered. Their approach was devoid of an understanding of what would best meet the needs of the people in the community the church was serving. I avoided, as did so many other pastors of growing churches, a concept of ministry that relied only upon the letter of The United Methodist *Discipline,* instead of its spirit. I demanded space for improvisation or innovation.

Here again, exclusive reliance upon Eurocentric cultural norms has done much to stifle, retard, and kill black churches in predominantly white denominations. It is axiomatic in African American culture that everything need not be done by the book. We see evidence of this compulsion in the development of American classical music, better known as jazz, which evolved out of the African American church.

Jazz is based in part on principles of spontaneity and innovation. Much of its development is rooted in oppositional expressions to European musical forms and cultural configurations. Although jazz intrinsically contains forms and patterns of European music, the main impetus of its development emerged out of the spontaneous, innovative impulses of African American artistic creativity. Jazz never could have developed without the freedom of spirit which translated and transcended the conventional forms and norms of European classical music.

Improvisation and *innovation,* according to the dictionary, simply refer to the ability to create, make, or do with the materials at hand, on the spur of the moment, to fill an unforeseen, immediate need. The spiritual life of black people has always embraced the notion of God or Spirit, endowed with the power to transform or change directions of the lives of God's people in the "twinkling of an eye."

Prophetic ministry and its biblical precedents also embody the notion of spontaneity and improvisation. The prophet may announce his proclamation from a written text, but invariably leaves space for an additional Word that may come from the Lord through direct experience. The prophet knows what he is to say, but is invariably open to the Spirit coming from on high to impart and empower his words.

Black culture and life have always valued the gift of improvisation. One preacher recalling his childhood made the following observation:

> Black people have always been able to improvise. I remember my mother was the best improviser I ever knew. She could take a pot of beans and make them seven different ways each day of the week. The amazing thing about my mother was that those beans would taste seven different ways each time she made them.[4]

The gift of improvisation is closely related to the propensity for freedom. The desire to do, create, and express unique styles of worship and to develop meaningful patterns of social and spiritual interaction are elements inherent in the black church and African American life and culture.

The following questions might be relative to the norms of improvisation and spontaneity: Is there a freedom of spirit which allows for the growth of spontaneity in our church? Is there an element of improvisation, in which programs, ministries, attitudes, and interactions accommodate the immediate and unforeseen presentation of needs and aspirations of parishioners? How much flexibility does the church possess in communicating ideas, attitudes, and feelings? Are we able to change directions, create new models and idioms consistent with black culture, or do we do everything according to the book or the prescribed norms of Euro-American culture? How open are we to new ideas and programs? How much freedom and latitude is given the congregation to present new ideas and opportunities for ministry?

Again, what's critical here is the cultivation of an ethos of openness, when people dare to create and devise, in accordance with perceived and real needs. Some norms of Euro-American culture are necessary and helpful for the growth of black churches, such as the concern for order, brevity, rationality, and consistency, and the value of stabilizing structures for intergenerational ministry.

But certainly, spontaneous and improvisational content without form can also be disastrous. The black church, for the sake of improvisation, can find itself upstream without a paddle if reverence for form and structure does not accompany the need to improvise and innovate. While improvisation and spontaneity are kingpins of African American culture, respect for order and form is equally important in planning and building the black church.

We have mentioned adaptive and expressive needs: the capacity to adapt to life as it is reveals myriad possibilities; the expression of sentiment in the process of adaptation. Both these needs are closely related to improvisation and spontaneity. The extent to which these forms of communal life are expressed freely in the realm of the church's life is a key indicator for potential growth. Such modes are consistent with the dynamic, passionate, expressive elements of African American culture.

If a black church simulates the experience of freedom congruent with black cultural norms and assumptions, it can truly grow. If the black church can accommodate the *law of the moment* as well as the *laws of permanency,* the possibilities for expansion remain extant. If black churches can follow both the text and the context of ministry, synthesize the dynamics and structures of black church life and culture, it can experience phenomenal growth. A further example of the importance of improvisation is related in the following story:

> Because the educational ministry of his church was floundering, a minister decided to implement a Rites of Passage program for black youth. Prior to its establishment, Sunday school enrollment had dropped and teacher morale accordingly dissipated. It wasn't until the minister improvised by establishing the Imani Institute in the educational program that the Sunday school enrollment increased and the educational ministry of the church experienced phenomenal growth. When the youth of the church began to undergo a transformation in perspective about themselves, their heritage and culture, and began to integrate these with the precepts of the Christian faith, the prophetic basis of the church's growth was accordingly established.[5]

The key here was improvisation and innovation. While the text, or discipline of the church, called for the establishment of a viable educational program, it did not recommend the establishment of a Rites of Passage program for black youth. The *text* called for education; the *context* required that Christian education be made relevant to the needs and concerns of black youth as they struggle with the critical issues of life. Improvisation, spontaneity, and innovation were essential in allowing the freedom to create something new. The result was increased growth. The church school grew from 20 to more then 100 in two years because of the contextual application of specific educational and cultural principles consistent with African American life and culture.

SPIRIT-CENTERED REALITY

Earlier, we mentioned the transcendent value of spiritual truth which compels the believer to go beyond the established parameters of conventional beliefs and formulas, the focus on a spirit-centered reality which creates the possibilities of communal and self-transcendence.

A God- and Spirit-centered life recognizes the existence of a higher power or entity which directs and shapes the paths of all who exist. Black culture highly affirms the existence of God, the ever-presence of the omnipotent, omniscient, all- and ever-knowing God who exacts justice and offers redemption amid the forces of injustice and annihilation.

Whatever notions of God persist, the idea and belief in a God who liberates, redeems, heals, and justifies black existence in America is an important construct in prophetic ministry and an indispensable component of black church growth.

Above all, the God of the African American experience is one who requires justice, shows mercy, and embraces God's people. This great Spirit, this all-enveloping love, serves as a source of redemptive empowerment for a people who have been all but severed from the mainstream of American society. When humankind errs and oppresses, annihilates and destroys, the Spirit will somehow bring stasis and equilibrium to the established order and those who suffer.

The prophetic church, utilizing the positive norms of black culture, espouse the God of individual and communal justice, whose ultimate concern is the liberation and well-being of the downtrodden and oppressed.

Further questions are pertinent here: Does the God we love and serve require of us justice, liberation, and mercy? Is the church willing to call into question those structures of individual and communal violence, disintegration, alienation, and fragmentation which destroy the people's resolve to live with dignity, humility, and vitality? To what extent does the church's ministry embody the principles of empowerment and evoke within believers the capacity for personal and social transformation?

These questions not only confront prophetic black churches, but are at the heart of black culture itself. The concern for spiritual, vocational, material, and communal well-being shapes all spiritual and ecclesial striving.

Without transcendence, which flows from a spirit-centered understanding of reality, the black church cannot surmount the structural, attitudinal, and relational impediments which stifle growth and stagnate life.

Being spiritually centered and spirit-filled are important dimensions of black church life. Nothing is more problematic than a church which possesses no enthusiasm for the gospel or joy for the ministry. One essential criteria for the growth of black churches is the manifestation of a joyous, celebrative spirit that reaffirms the meaning and purpose of life.

This Holy Spirit is also an emblem of African American culture and permeates black life. A certain aliveness and rhythm pulsates in black communities. Visit black neighborhoods in any major metropolis, and one discovers the presence of a particular Spirit or Soul that embodies the essence of black life in America. Duke Ellington captured it with these words: "It don't mean a thing if it ain't got that swing."

Joseph L. White, in his monumental study *The Psychology of Blacks*, put it this way:

> The African world view begins with a holistic conception of the human condition. The human organism is conceived as a totality made up of interlocking systems. This total person is simultaneously a feeling, experiencing, sensualizing, sensing and knowing human being living in a dynamic, vitalistic world where everything is inter-related and endowed with supreme force of life. There is a sense of aliveness, intensity and animation in the music, dance, song, language and lifestyles of Africans. Emotions are not labelled as bad; therefore, there is no need to repress feelings of compassion, joy or sensuality.[6]

A spirit-centered reality has often helped blacks to transcend and survive the racism and mistreatment by both white oppressors and black reactionaries. To grow prophetically, the black church must have within its theology an understanding of this spirit-centered reality and its meaning for black existence.

Several other positive norms of black culture are essential for prophetic church growth: *Resilience and revitalization, coping with oppression; mastery of language and the oral tradition, valuing direct experience; respect for matriarchal and patriarchal authority; maintaining cultural and racial continuity; promoting communal solidarity and collective consciousness; and the primacy of male-female relationships.*[7]

Black cultural norms revolve around issues of interdependence, interrelatedness, connectedness, and synthesis.[8]

Understanding the psychological, spiritual, and social needs of African American people is a feasible starting point for building churches. Once these needs and cultural assumptions are fathomed, one can begin the process of developing a church by utilizing twelve prophetic principles in the four major areas of church life: *Worship, Pastoral Care, Education,* and *Evangelism.*

Three Principles of Prophetic Worship

W e have described the biblical foundations of prophetic church growth by emphasizing the four aspects of biblical prophecy: *passion or compassion, conviction, investment,* and *vision.* These four elements constitute the foundation of prophetic church growth in African American churches and should be cornerstones in the development of ministries that speak to the spiritual needs and culture of African American people.

We also listed the positive norms of African American culture which should help ministers and evangelists establish a coherent and viable basis for doing ministry with black people. Let us now turn our attention to the various areas of the church's ministry where prophetic principles can be feasibly instituted in order to effect church growth.

One of the most important dimensions of the church's ministry is the experience of worship. In fact, in the majority of cases, a person's first contact with a church is through its Sunday or mid-week worship service. It is in this context that individuals often make assessments about the vitality, relevance, character, and spirit of a particular congregation. The experience of worship tells much about the people of the congregation, their nature and temperament, their sincerity, and their consistency in relating to others' understandings of God. People who visit churches for the first time, as they struggle with the meaning of life and death and attempt to make sense out of the ultimate concerns of their lives, look for a particular feeling of worship which creates a sense of belonging.

Those who are looking for a church to join will ask a series of questions of the worship experience: How do I feel about what I am seeing and experiencing in the worship service? Do I sense warmth and belonging from the people here, or do I feel like an outsider? Does the worship service meet the deeper yearnings of my spirit? Is the preaching creative, dynamic, and informative? Is the singing and music inspirational? In other words, does the worship service communicate passion? Do the sermons convey conviction? Are the people of this congregation truly invested in the experience of worship? Can I catch sight of a larger vision, which both empowers and compels full participation in the glory of God and the celebration of the Kingdom?

The experience of worship is key in winning souls to Christ and in building vital congregations through the use of prophetic principles. Three principles are essential for prophetic worship:

1. The worship experience should *celebrate* life in Christ.

2. The worship event should *invite* people into the fellowship of believers.

3. The worship service should *inform* people about God's wondrous and creative activity in the world.

CELEBRATION

Celebrate means to "observe with ceremonies of respect, festivity or rejoicing. To extol and praise." Prophetic worship buoyantly celebrates life in all its manifestations and fullness; it displays the gifts of the Holy Spirit. It passionately witnesses to the glory, honor, mercy, love, joy, and peace of Jesus Christ. This celebration not only involves the expression of feeling within the context of worship, but offers sentiment which conveys meaning; it reaches out to others and creates a sense of belonging and a sharing of common goals, values, and aspirations.

Churches often don't grow because their worship services are dry, lifeless, devoid of the passion and enthusiasm for the celebration of life that the Holy Spirit creates.

It is difficult to envision the biblical prophets without passion and a heightened expectation for celebrating the new, dynamic, and creative possibilities of God as revealed in the lives of God's people and the larger covenant community. While prophetic diatribes against the nation of Israel were more caustic than celebratory, the main course of the prophetic message contained elements of celebration.

Does your experience of worship joyfully celebrate life through Christ? Does the mood, style, ethos, language, music, preaching, teaching, and overall ambience of worship celebrate the creative, dynamic, transformative power of God? Does that celebration convey passion, conviction, investment, and vision? Do people feel a sense of belonging, yearning, and sharing as they collectively witness to the love and grace of God working in their lives?

The principle of celebration in prophetic worship means that the celebrants experience, elicit, and explore the full spectrum of human sentiment, allowing people to express themselves through sorrow, tears, joy, or laughter. The apex of the prophetic worship experience is the realization of our humanity and divinity, our mortality and eternity through the creative, dynamic exploration and celebration of our life through Christ. It is precisely in the discovery of our humanity in all its fullness, its range of probabilities and possibilities, its successes and failures, its joys and disappointments, its agonies and ecstasies, that prophetic worship is most able to confer upon people a sense of ultimate meaning and belonging to God. Community is invariably established through the collective celebration of the story which binds our lives together.

The point of prophetic worship is to place people in touch with those transformative elements of meaning which give life new direction, purpose, vitality, and strength. The celebration of life in the context of worship is an important prophetic growth principle, if people are to be reached at the center of their lives.

A creative, dynamic worship experience is essential for reaching the unchurched and winning them to Christ, because it speaks of vitality and aliveness. People need to sense the pulsations, rhythms, joys, and jubilation of life in Christ. Celebrative, exhilarating worship moves people toward positive transformation.

Many people often observe that when depressed and debased in spirit, they go to churches where the worship experience is inspiring, rejuvenating, and transforming so that sorrow is dissipated, doubt dispelled, and existing barriers between them and God are eliminated. People today need an experience of worship which will celebrate the Good News of Christ. The world is full of bad news and the search is on for churches which will celebrate life in a way that surpasses the fervor and zeal of fans at sports arenas and concert halls.

THE FOUR MOVEMENTS
OF CELEBRATIVE WORSHIP

Four basic elements are essential in creating a celebrative worship format.

1. Inspiration

A celebrative worship experience should inspire people to move closer to Christ. It should demonstrate the various ways this can be done. It should arouse curiosity and challenge people to creatively engage in a critical examination and celebration in every aspect of their lives. Inspirational worship services succeed in lifting the spirits of those cast down, mending broken hearts, easing troubled minds, and revitalizing vanquished spirits.

The Good News of Christ is a message of hope and should engage people on levels which bring meaning to them. The Good News inspires people to deal with life's changes and to effect the kinds of changes that will bring about personal wholeness and fulfillment.

All the preaching, singing, praying, and teaching of the Sunday worship experience should contain elements of inspiration. Does the sermon inspire people to constructive spiritual action? Does the singing lift spirits and exude joy for life in Christ? Does the praying reach people at the nucleus of their human and spiritual experience? Does the language and tone of preaching, singing, praying, and teaching equally inspire people to remove those impediments which thwart the full realization of God? These are essential questions for those seeking to develop more inspirational worship services.

One preacher related the story of the trials he experienced in revitalizing worship services at his new charge. Tradition had entrenched itself and the choirs of the church sang only anthems. When the issue of gospel music was introduced, the members of the various choirs rejected the idea. Responses ranged from "We don't sing that kind of music here" to "Gospel music is too emotional." This minister happened to be serving a mainstream denomination black church in a predominantly black middle-income community. While the choirs prided themselves on singing anthems, which were good music, the pews on Sundays were only partially full because the music lacked inspiration.

Anthems as well as the classics are very inspirational music. Few things are as exhilarating as Bach's B Minor Mass, Handel's *Messiah,* or the choral arrangements of Beethoven or Hayden. However, to appeal to the younger segments of the community in which it was located, the church had to develop a worship format that included more inspirational, spiritual, and gospel music. After adding a good inspirational gospel choir, worship attendance began to increase. Now the church is full on Sundays.[1]

We stated earlier that one of the positive norms of African American culture is the need for the free-flowing expression of ideas, passions, and feelings. The prophetic worship experience that would be celebrative and inspirational must contain norms and values which speak to the psychic, spiritual, and emotional needs of African American people. The worship experience must be inspirational if it is to succeed in winning black people to Christ. It must, in other words, speak not only to the mind, but to the soul.

If your worship services lack inspiration and vitality, what changes can you implement to make them more fervent? How can you educate parishioners to the need for making such changes? See the checklist at the end of this chapter for suggestions. A process of education and information must occur if the congregation will support moving away from traditional norms and styles into new frontiers. To enable your church to grow prophetically, you must develop a celebrative worship service which inspires and uplifts the people of God.

2. Valuation

What values are reflected through the experience of worship? The answers range from the aesthetics and ambience of the sanctuary to the quality of music and content of the sermon. The dictionary defines *valuation* as "an estimation of or appreciation of the worth, merit or character of something."

The what, how, when, and where of worship say much about the priorities and values of a particular congregation. For example, people who visit worship for the first time will scrutinize everything from the style of dress to the type of hospitality shown them by parishioners. All these things, however elementary and mundane they seem, are important aspects of the valuation process in the worship experience.

I shall never forget the story related by a clergy friend about the reaction of his upper-middle-class congregation when a homeless person came to worship, stretched out on a pew, and snored loudly through the entire service. The members' reaction of utter dismay, horror, and contempt said much about the values of their church.

Subsequent to this "outrageous occurrence," as it was termed by some members, the stewards recommended that a particular door through which this homeless person wandered be padlocked, in the event of any future "intrusions by other street people."[2]

This reaction to an "intruder" in worship said much about the values of the congregation. It was later discovered that many visitors in the church that day were highly offended by the reaction of the members and never returned. While the worship experience lacked vitality and enthusiasm, the problem was further exacerbated by the repulsion of good Christians toward one of the "have nots."

Valuation is a critical process of the celebrative worship experience. People often make value assessments about the life and attitudes of the church based on their observations in worship. The attitudes of parishioners also reflect specific values. If the church is in an upheaval because a homeless person visits worship service, what does this say about the overall attitude of the church toward the least of these, of whom Jesus so pointedly speaks? It is the duty of all Christians to minister to the dispossessed in society.

Responses to such situations are often an indication of true Christian values.

To what issues does the sermon speak? What repertoires of music are utilized in worship? Does worship utilize the vast, rich, and varied reservoirs of sacred music from the African American experience, or is there a general contempt and disdain for such things? The refusal to acknowledge the value, sanctity, and worth of African American culture and creativity says much about the values of the church itself. For many would-be members, this certainly does not encourage a celebration of black culture, which should be a hallmark of the African American church.

If there are important issues in the life of the community in which the church is located, there should be something in worship which values those concerns as people seek answers to the critical issues facing them. Critical concerns that involve the lives of people in the pew also should be addressed through the medium and idioms of the worship experience. It is essential to the celebrative, inspirational, prophetic forms of worship to prioritize the issues, grounds of meaning, and matters of ultimate concern in people's lives.

3. Consecration

The profaneness of the world, the desacralization which occurs at the core of human existence and eviscerates a sense of the holy, often anesthetizes people to the reality of God. People are seeking recovery of a sense of the sacred. They want assurance that life has ultimate spiritual value and meaning. They have exhausted their search in the world and have encountered utter meaninglessness. Now more than ever, they seek a restoration of confidence, of vital connectedness with the holy, high, transcendent ground of human existence.

It is through realizing the holy and its envelopment of their lives, that human spiritual awareness is transformed and a spirit of celebration and joy for the gift of life is wholly expressed in the context of worship.

When asked why she shouted on Sunday mornings, Sister Sadie Jones simply said, "When I think about how good God has been to me and for me, how he saved my life and drug me out of the fiery pit of hell, I can't help but shout, brother!"

Experiencing the transcendent through an encounter with the holy through a process of consecration is essential to prophetic worship. Barriers are broken down, the old moorings are replaced, and transcendent joy and power ensue in the life of the believer.

The prophets of old invariably had a sense of the sacred. They understood their prophetic office to be consecrated by God and were compelled to prophesy the truth to the people of God. Prophetic worship, in seeking to consecrate the lives of God's people, and in pointing the way to the higher reality, should disseminate the truth of human existence in ways which effect positive transformation.

Consecration means "the process of making clean" and involves a candid recognition of spiritual, psychological, existential, and ethical truth in the lives of the people of God. What truths does the experience of worship exemplify? Does the sermon speak truthfully to the critical issues of our times and the ultimate issues of people's lives?

In making decisions about joining a particular congregation, many people often ask how the experience of worship speaks to the central truths of their lives. Consecrated worship goes far in propagating the truth of our human condition and discloses the reality of the sacred which people seek to reestablish in their search for meaning, wholeness, and vitality.

Does the experience of worship in your church point people toward the sacred and the holy? Is there a process of consecration which empowers and encourages people to face the central and ultimate issues of their lives? To what extent does the process of consecration facilitate an awareness of the transcendent, an awareness which ultimately leads to the prophetic transformation of human experience? Consecration is indispensable in the celebration of prophetic worship.

4. Motivation

If the worship inspires, valuates, and consecrates persons, it also must motivate them to participate in those realities and processes which will effect a constructive transformation of their spiritual lives. What should prophetic worship motivate them to do?

First, individuals should be motivated to return to the church for worship. This will largely depend upon how the person was inspired, challenged, valued, and consecrated during a previous experience of worship.

Second, if the person returns for worship, he or she should be motivated to reflect critically on the Word of God and its meaning and relevancy to his or her own life.

Third, individuals experiencing worship should be challenged or motivated to engage in some constructive activity which will facilitate positive spiritual transformation in their lives. The first step in accepting the need for positive transformation is to attend a worship experience where the beneficent, transcendent reality of God can be authentically experienced. The next step is to join a church that will facilitate knowledge of both the imperatives and the savoir faire of creative and positive transformation.

In summarizing the four movements of celebrative worship, we stated that individuals who are potential members usually have their first exposure to the church through the worship service. To encourage people to join a particular congregation, the forms of worship must do at least four essential things:

1. It must *inspire* people through the dispensation of the Good News. Such inspiration must be done in accordance with the cultural norms and presuppositions of the African American community.

2. It must *value* human life and prioritize those issues of ultimate concern which critically affect people at the core of their lives.

3. It must speak to the reality of spiritual truth through a *consecration* process which places people in immediate awareness of a sense of the sacred.

4. And it must *motivate* them to reflect critically upon the Word of God as it is revealed in their lives, and compel them to engage in the transformative processes which will effect positive spiritual change. Being motivated to join a particular church is one step toward spiritual transformation.

INVITATION

The next principle of prophetic worship is *invitation*. In order to increase the growth of the African American church utilizing prophetic principles, the worship service must invite people to participate in celebrating life through Christ. It also must invite them to belong to the community of faith by encouraging them to engage in critical reflection upon the meaning and purpose of the possibilities of life in that community.

A great tragedy of Christianity today, and a deterrent to black church growth, is the church's failure to invite people to belong to the fellowship of believers. Too often, a church is guided by a "members only" philosophy and fails to challenge people to participate in the celebration of Christ and his Kingdom. The Christian church has been accused of being an elitist institution whose outreach is limited to "card-carrying members." Many stories have been related about the ways church members shut off potential members by everything from being impervious to ideas from new and potential members to "owning a pew" and not allowing visitors to sit there.

I recall one incident in which a long-standing member refused to give up her pew to a visitor and, upon the pastor's request that she "show some Christian courtesy to our visitors," proceeded after service to "bless out" the pastor for his indiscretion.[3] Attitudes of possessiveness and selfishness as exemplified in the church often alienate people who are looking for a church home. Perhaps this is the exception more than the rule, but quite often the church manifests a country-club attitude to potential members, thus alienating them permanently.

The worship experience may be the only opportunity for the church to make an impression on a visitor who is looking for a church to join. Invitation is an essential element in facilitating a sense of belonging for those seeking a closer relationship with God. How does the worship service extend an invitation to participate in both the worship service and the church?

First, the *dynamics and form* of the worship service must create a context for participation. Is the ethos cultivated in the service inviting or repressive, hostile or generous and benevolent? What are the attitudes of those participating in and conducting the service? Do they exemplify an attitude of friendliness? Are visitors sincerely welcomed and affirmed? Does the experience of worship create a climate of friendship, openness, and genuine concern for others? If a visitor says "Amen," do parishioners lose composure by verbally or facially conveying contempt for such outbursts? The dynamics and form of the worship experience should invite full participation in the service.

One friend related an experience which now seems rather amusing. Feeling tired and depressed, he sought out worship in a well-known mainline denominational church while visiting Philadelphia on an extended work assignment. As the pastor approached the climax of his sermon, the congregation sat in stone cold silence, but my friend jumped up and shouted at the top of his lungs, "Hallelujah! Thank you, Jesus!" Members of the congregation were so startled, they stared him into silence during the remainder of the service. Even the pastor was so surprised that he lost his place and was visibly frayed.

Second, does the pastor invite people to participate in the service? Does the sermon encourage, in the words of Ted Jennings, a critical reflection upon the Christian mythos? The sermon is often a critical gauge of the pastor's relationship with the congregation. The apostle Paul exhorted the young Timothy in carrying out his pastoral duties to "reprove, rebuke and exhort in season and out of season." The trouble is that many pastors spend too much time in the pulpit grinding personal axes, scolding and castigating the people because of some past wrong or indiscretion. One young man who joined our church had defected from another because, in his words, "The pastor spent too much time beating up on his parishioners from the pulpit."[4] The sermon and the personality of the pastor are indispensable in creating a climate of invitation. Airing the congregation's dirty linen from the pulpit too frequently can discourage visitors from joining.

In surveying the biblical precedents, we often see the prophet issuing a clarion call for critical reflection upon current conditions and future life under God. Although the prophet admonishes by utilizing the language of reprimand and reproach in calling the people back to God, he nevertheless invites people to reflect upon the meaning and trajectories of personal faith.

Prophetic language often conveys unconditional imperatives for reestablishing a relationship with God, but always the objective is to invite people to participate in rebuilding community through the reestablishment of the covenant. The sermon therefore must demand, but also invite full participation in the experience of worship and the celebration of life through Christ.

Many mainline denominations have lost potential black members due in part to styles of worship of black congregations, and this problem with style has extended to the preaching. While many blacks seek worship that is dynamic and enthusiastic, and invokes active participation in both the services and life of the church, their spirits often are dampened by sermons that are less spirited or which emulate the Eurocentric and North American religious traditions. Black people generally do not prefer a sermon that is hushed and pacific, serene and beatific.

Generalizations are difficult to apply everywhere. Many white southerners in mainline denominations have the more fervent worship traditions reminiscent of the African American spiritual tradition. On the other hand, many blacks do not prefer such enthusiastic modes of worship but instead desire a more reticent, less emotional worship experience.

A hallmark of the African American spiritual tradition not always practiced by their Euro-American counterparts is the celebration of a hymn of invitation after the sermon. Here the preacher extends an opportunity for those worshiping to unite with the church. This is an open call to become part of the congregation. It is useful because it encourages people to enter into a partnership with God and the church. As a widespread practice across Protestantism, when an invitation to join the church is issued, people sense that their presence in the ongoing life of the congregation can make a difference. There should be something in the experience of worship that facilitates and precipitates a willingness to join the church.

The worship experience is an invitation to live life through Christ. Celebration of the sacraments is an invitation to fellowship with Christ, to experience the fullness of life which only God can give.

Other concerns of invitation center around the milieu and ambience of the church and sanctuary. Every nuance, from the color of the carpet to the banners that embellish the sanctuary walls, speak to the issue of invitation. Few people would unite with a church whose ambience is unclean.

Does your church invite? Does the atmosphere of the sanctuary impel people to Christ? Is the carpeting a warm color? Does the color of the walls elicit ingathering and fellowship? Is the overall feeling consistent with creating a sense of belonging? What about vestments, paraments, and other symbols of worship? Do they convey warmth, fellowship, and invitation?

I remember when one trustee and I engaged in lengthy discussion about the importance of the church conveying a positive, responsible image in the community. For one year, I had tried desperately to motivate the trustees to replace the fluorescent bulbs in our outside church sign. Finally, after no results, I explained the importance of the church serving as the light of God among humanity. Until I was able to metaphorically draw analogies between physical and spiritual light, I couldn't get lights in our outside sign.

Moreover, the critical issue here was the image of invitation which the church was giving to the larger community. What do people think when in passing a church at night, they see no lights in the outdoor sign? The lack of outside light was correlated, in my mind, with the absence of spiritual light inside the church. How is the church to help people find their way out of the darkness if its lights are burned out? Something as simple as inoperable lights discourages visitation because it says that there is no life inside; no one is home.

In short, an extinguished church sign issues no *invitation* to come and experience life in the church. Everything about the physical structure of the church and, more important, the ethos of the worship service should invite people into fellowship. In these times when people so easily excuse themselves from participation in the church, congregations must be challenged to find ways to become more inviting.

Let me illustrate this another way. Have you ever visited a city for the first time alone and felt uncomfortable in the hotel where you were staying? Usually hotels have a hospitality suite. Here there are no strangers, but only after you visit this suite do you begin to comfortably acclimate yourself to your surroundings.

The church should be the hospitality suite of society, where no strangers exist and all are welcome. The worship service should invite and create a sense of belonging and hospitality for those who would seek God. Does your worship experience create an invitation to celebrate and belong?

One creative idea established in the church I now serve—the *Sunday greeters*—promotes a feeling of belonging. The people of Hope Church work faithfully to make all visitors and members feel at home. A spirit of warmth and acceptance is created on Sundays. Weekday meetings are spiced with humor, healing, and the cultivation of a family atmosphere. A frequent statement is made by Hope members: "There are no strangers here. We are all the family of God." Accordingly, there is a concerted effort on behalf of the membership to extend themselves in service to others. "It's not that we go *out of our way*. It *is* our way," remarked one member.[5]

INFORMATION

The third principle of prophetic worship essential to the growth of viable African American congregations is *information*. In modern society, we think of information as being associated with and disbursed through technosystems. Computers expedite information at the touch of a button. Global events are flashed to us in seconds by satellite through intricate technology. Bundles of information are stored in microchips and disseminated in milliseconds.

But while science conveys information about humanity's technical and scientific capabilities, worship is the principal medium for conveying information about our relationship with God.

Worship is primarily an informational arena. It imparts vital knowledge about humanity's understanding of itself, and about God's creative and wondrous workings in the universe through the lives of the people.

The average person experiencing worship is asking, "So what? What does this mean for my life? Is this something new in the telling of this story? What will this worship service or sermon tell me that I don't already know? What preexistent or new truths borne out by personal experience will be corroborated by the experience of worship?"

The information of vital prophetic worship should distinguish itself from the information propagated through conventional media sources. It should place hearers in intimate touch with knowledge that leads to positive, personal transformation. It should tell them what's right with their lives, instead of what's always wrong, and how personal change can be dynamically effected. Leave the bad news to the secular media; the church should announce Good News!

The biblical prophets announced an effective message because they had the ability to incite the anticipation of new knowledge and information for the people of God. Often the prophets conveyed words and phrases that had been previously heard. Yet, contained within the expectation of the hearers was a feeling that something new, fresh, exciting, and compelling would be spoken. This new knowledge inspired the progressive alteration of personal faith.

A word from God should contain something new. It would provide the people with a more intimate prescript for moving closer to God. In the words of Francis Bacon, "Knowledge is power," and worship should become a medium for the prophetic dispensation of new information and knowledge. Personal, social, and spiritual transformation are the keys here, and information should aid in their realization.

This need for something new does not mean that old stories cannot be told in old ways, that traditions of worship and corresponding interpretations cannot be practiced. It does mean that in the context of modernity, the worship experience provides the forum in which radically new information about human spiritual possibilities are explicated.

This knowledge, shared in the form of vital information, must contain prescripts for developing an enduring faith. People today are seeking not so much an exposition of faith, for they are aware of its nature and aspects, but an understanding of how to acquire it and apply it in their present lives.

Countless times in my encounters with people, I have heard that the worship services do not inspire or inform; that while the preacher tells familiar stories in familiar ways, nothing new is said that will challenge and exhort hearers.

The sermon, as with much of Protestant worship that has not been biased toward a European form of eucharistic worship, is the culminating part of worship in the black Protestant tradition. To maintain its importance, the black sermon must not only inspire but inform. The preacher must find ways to hone and expand his or her knowledge of Scripture. The scope should be multidisciplinary, and the preacher should be a keen observer of life itself.

The orator takes his cue from *inspiration;* the preacher and prophet take theirs from *revelation.* But the Word of God, conveyed prophetically in worship, should emanate from both. In hearing the Word, people should be inspired to enter into life with Christ, and to have equally revealed to them the practical ways such communion can be achieved.

Not every sermon is designed to transform or inspire. The preacher, however great, will not hit the mark every week with every parishioner. But he or she should have a reputation for bringing *fresh, exciting, exhilarating, inspiring,* and *revealing* sermons to the people of God. Gardner Taylor once said, during the Beecher Lectures at Yale Divinity School, that if one were to find the cause of death of the Christian church, one would discover that the sermon had killed it.

The tragedy of modern Christianity is the lack of diligent preparation by pastors in developing and delivering the Sunday sermon. Sermons often lack drive, conviction, inspiration, and dedication. They fail to reveal information that will challenge people to conceptualize and reconfigure old truths in new ways, thus bringing about personal transformation. Often, the content of those sermons is without biblical basis, nor is it rooted in existential truth. The delivery is frequently stale and wooden.

In the black church, the key to winning souls to Christ is that the *manner* and *matter,* the *content* and *delivery,* must lift, invoke, provoke, and inspire people in creative ways. Just as there is no thief like a bad book, there is no robber like a boring, uninviting, uninvested preacher who disinterestedly purveys platitudes and robs the people of their time, sanity, and interest.

In reviewing the proclamations of the prophets, again we see language that is buoyant and colorful, words that incite, inspire, amuse, and amaze; deliveries that are passionate and moving, eliciting both joy and anger, confirmation and contempt. We see messages that "comfort the afflicted and afflict the comfortable."

Are your sermons a source of new information to the people of God? Do they *reveal* information which empowers people to move closer to Christ? Do they affirm the present but point to the future? In hearing your sermons, can people gain knowledge of how to *practically apply* the precepts of the faith in order to realize their potential and better their lives? Do your sermons reveal the reality of God and inspire people to participate in that reality?

Theoretically, prophetic preaching can range from mercy and love to the salvation and liberation of the beloved community. How is God saving the people? How is God liberating the people from various forms of enslavement? How might one experience God's everlasting love and mercy in tough and troubled times?

In worship, the *music, language,* and *tones of human interaction* also are vital sources of information for the prophetic church. *What* people do and say in worship is just as important as *how* they do and say it. We mentioned earlier the importance of human interaction. Does the music inspire and inform? Do the members and participants in the church's worship service inspire and inform as they celebrate life in Christ?

CHECKLIST AND SUMMARY OF PROPHETIC WORSHIP PRINCIPLES

Celebration

Principle One: The church must *celebrate* life through Christ. It must celebrate the positive norms and styles of the Afrocentric worship experience through the manifestation of four primary modes of expression and interpretation.

The first mode is *inspiration.* Any celebration of worship in the prophetic tradition should be inspiring. It should encourage people to develop a closer relationship with Christ. It should inspire a critical examination of their lives in every aspect so as to remove those impediments precluding the realization of human potential and the actualization of a full partnership with God. Spirits should be lifted through the celebration of music, fellowship, preaching, and praying. Inspiration is a cornerstone of worship celebration.

Inspiration Checklist

What can I do to make the worship services of our church more celebrative and inspiring?

____A. Evaluate the existing order of worship to determine whether its current structure is optimally geared toward celebrative worship;

____B. Evaluate the litanies, prayers, and other components of your worship service to determine viability. Do the current elements convey vibrance and enthusiasm?

____C. Develop training sessions for all the participants, including liturgists, worship leaders, Scripture readers, announcers, and others who regularly participate in worship;

____D. Develop and strengthen the inspirational choir(s). Develop a variety of repertoire. Emphasize quality singing and preparation;

____E. Change the focus, mode, and content of sermons and sermon delivery by making them more relevant to people's experiences. Preach Good News with vitality, life, and enthusiasm;

____F. Evaluate the ethos and ambience of your sanctuary. Does it need refurbishing? Do walls need to be painted, banners mounted? Do the participants of worship dress appropriately? Are they neat, clean, and convey warmth and joy?

____G. Change instruments of music to create an atmosphere more conducive to celebration in the black tradition.

Envision the type of worship experience you desire to create and dare to implement that vision. Create an atmosphere of worship where people can celebrate life through Christ through the affirmation of their culture and spiritual traditions. Don't be afraid to try new modes of worship, incorporate new songs and prayers, and prepare different kinds of sermons, from the narrative to the expository! Celebrative worship should include the following:

1. An atmosphere that is friendly and inviting (there are no visitors or strangers at any worship setting);

2. Designated greeters or shepherds whose primary purpose is to make visitors feel welcome (greeters could follow up with a call or visit to new people);

3. Participants who are dressed appropriately and manifest a helpful, courteous, and friendly demeanor (greeters, ushers, acolytes, worship leaders—all should exude warmth and cheer);

4. Cultivation of an order of service which facilitates the worship process and the feeling of belonging;

5. Prayers, sermons, songs, and testimonials which inspire and uplift the people of God (an atmosphere of love, hope, and joy should be established);

6. A moment for children, or a children's sermon which conveys the core message of the proclamation;

7. Invitation for all to join fellowship after worship service;

8. Quarterly evaluation of existing worship format:

> Do our services tell others that we are a friendly church?
> What percentage of our visitors return for worship?
> Do our services convey life, enthusiasm, joy, love?
> Do our participants convey friendliness and caring?
> Does the congregation convey warmth and friendliness to new people?

The second mode of celebrative worship is *valuation*. The experience of worship exemplifies the values and concerns of particular congregations. Those experiencing worship for the first time obtain a sense of their own value and worth as co-participants in the process. In the experience of worship, people must thereby get a sense that life through Christ is of the highest value and benefit, and that it relates to them in their areas of ultimate concern.

Valuation Checklist

What values are conveyed through our worship services? How can we convey to people through worship that their well-being and presence is of the highest concern to God and to the congregation? How can we tell them that life as valued through the experience of Christ will ultimately, creatively, and positively transform their lives?

___A. Create a worship format that is inclusive. Incorporate children's sermons. Establish time in which visitors can be welcomed, greeted, and invited to fellowship. Create a milieu in which all people can feel a sense of belonging;

___B. Create a context for worship in which the ethos, traditions, folkways, and mores of African American culture are unequivocally celebrated and valued; songs, prayers, and sermons should reflect the vitality and ethnicity of African American culture;

___C. Develop the various components of worship, from the choirs to the preaching, in a way that will speak to the ultimate values and concerns of people in the pew;

___D. Establish a climate of genuine human caring, wherein strangers feel welcomed and will want to return to your church.

An "Ideal" Order of Worship

Prelude
Processional Hymn
Call to Worship
Invocation
Hymn of Praise
A Time of Sharing
    Announcements
    Welcome and Greeting to Visitors
    Prayer Requests, Testimonials
    Witnessing of Concerns
Altar Calls and Pastoral Prayer
Choir Selection
Children's Sermon
Scripture Reading
Hymn of Preparation
The Proclamation
Hymn of Invitation
Offertory Prayer
Offertory

Choir Selection
Recessional Hymn
Benediction
Benediction Response
Postlude

The third vehicle of celebrating prophetic worship is *consecration*. Consecration restores to the individual a sense of the self as sacred and places the perceiver in a relationship of intimacy with the Holy. Worship in this context must point toward the holy ground of individual experience, as well as affirm the collective identity of persons celebrating life through the beloved community.

Worship of Christ through the affirmation and celebration of the Christian faith must thus have some consecrating dimension if it is to inspire people to become part of a local congregation.

> ### Consecration Checklist
>
> *In our celebration of worship, do people feel a sense of the sacred? Do the sermon, music, praying, and fellowship convey intimations of the presence of God? What does our experience of worship offer that will inform people that God is alive?*
>
> ____A. Develop a worship format and ethos which create a sense of the sacred;
>
> ____B. Utilize paraments, banners, vestments, and other symbols of worship which sacralize the experience of worship and give people a sense of the intimate and the ultimate;
>
> ____C. Deliver sermons which address the human need for the transcendent and speak to the timeless truths of the human condition;
>
> ____D. Develop an ethos that will compel people to examine the sacred within themselves and thus consecrate themselves for the Lord's work.

The fourth movement of celebrative worship is *motivation*. We said that the experience of worship should galvanize and petition people into making positive changes in their lives. There must be something in worship which encourages people to move closer to Christ. The objective is to shift people from the role of passive spectators of the life of the church to active participators in building the kingdom of God.

Motivation Checklist

____A. Develop a music ministry that is inspiring and multidimensional;

____B. Preach and teach to the central concerns of people's lives;

____C. Preach in ways that will arouse curiosity, inspire critical reflection, compel constructive action, create a desire to belong to the fellowship of Christ as represented in your particular congregation;

____D. Cultivate a worship style and format which reflects an abiding respect for the norms, values, and ethos of the African American experience. Make sure those norms, values, and ethos are unapologetically celebrative in the context of worship;

____E. Discover creative ways to reach people, holding their interest and motivating a return to your church.

Invitation

From celebration, we move to the second principle, *invitation*. The church should develop an open-door policy which invites, nurtures, and creates a sense of belonging for present and prospective members. Because the worship service is generally a person's first experience with a particular congregation, it must transmit an atmosphere of invitation, openness, and friendliness if people are to gain a sense of belonging.

Invitation Checklist

____A. In the liturgy and litany of worship, utilize language which exemplifies genuine caring and invites people to become a part of the congregation;

____B. Celebrate visitors and reach out to them, before, during, and after worship;

____C. Develop the proclamation or sermons which speak to the central issues on the critical needs of people in the pew;

____D. Develop music and other components of worship in the celebrative, invitational mode, and express a variety of repertoire;

____E. Implement a hymn of invitation or a call to discipleship after the sermon;

____F. Always stress hospitality, service, and the openness of the church to all persons, nonmembers as well as members. The worship experience, in every form and nuance, should be an invitation to fellowship, discipleship, and membership in the body of Christ.

Information

The third principle of prophetic worship is *information*. Worship should inspire people to apply the precepts and concepts of the faith through the consistent application of Christian principles.

Information Checklist

____A. Develop a worship format that creatively discloses information which will vitally impact people in the critical areas of their lives;

____B. Underscore the importance of sharing information and knowledge as a viable means of applying faith;

____C. Explore new motifs, paradigms, and presuppositions in exegesis and construction of sermons; make them a conduit for knowledge that will help people reconfirm the meaningful aspects of their lives.

CHAPTER FOUR

Three Principles of Prophetic Pastoral Care

If the worship service is the place where people make their initial decisions about whether to unite with a congregation, pastoral care is the function of leadership which helps to create a sense of belonging through unimpeded accessibility.

The quality of pastoral care offered is critical to prophetically increasing the black church, for people are seeking a place of refuge and healing from the wounds and hurts of daily life. They need nurture, care, and affirmation, a place to go to be heard, not ignored; fed, not starved. The *ability* of the pastor to preach and reach the hearts of people during worship is important. Equally significant is the pastor's *availability* beyond the Sunday worship experience.

When asked to what she attributed the phenomenal growth in the membership of her church, an elderly parishioner responded, "Our pastor. He really cares for us because he's always close by."[1]

It is true that being "always close by" can lead to clergy fatigue and burnout, but one essential criterion for growing churches is the pastor's accessibility to the existing and potential flock. We live in a society where abilities are glorified and availability is vilified. Availability without continuous presence is often what people are seeking from pastoral leadership.

Many larger churches are now aware of or facing the increasing problem of pastoral availability, manifested in such behavior as not going to the cemetery to bury parishioners after a funeral, or not visiting the sick and housebound. The issue is a critical one, and each leader must seriously weigh the consequences when developing prophetic models of church growth.

Even in the largest churches, the people of God must sense that they are cared for when they are facing life's most difficult challenges. They must know that the church truly loves and nurtures them, and will provide services to minister to their greatest and most perplexing needs.

A characteristic of the biblical prophets was their sense of concern for the people of Israel. Notwithstanding their vitriolic tongues, the sharp invectives inveighed against the people of God for apostasy and sin, they cared about the future of Israel and its people. Whatever judgment is leveled against a prophet, we know that the urgency and exigency of his message is steeped in an abiding concern for the welfare of God's people.

Seldom do we think of the prophets as agents of caring, commissioned to proclaim to the people the everlasting mercy and love of God. The image of the prophet as firebrand, railing against the ills of society, often overshadows the prophet as caretaker of souls—one called to be a *wounded healer* in the midst of personal and national calamities.[2]

The challenge of prophetic leadership is ultimately the restoration of full personhood and wholeness, which can occur only if the terms of the covenant are kept.

The pastor who engages in a prophetic style of ministry must utilize three basic principles for pastoral care. To build a viable congregation, he or she must serve as the *clarifier, restorer-comforter,* and *creative confronter* of the people of God.

THE PASTOR AS PROPHETIC CLARIFIER

The pastor who does not find church growth incompatible with prophetic leadership must serve as the *clarifier* of the vision and mission of the church in the lives of God's people. He or she must also, through pastoral care and counseling, make clear the paths to the faith, revealing those areas of people's lives where God's redemptive, salvific work is taking place.

In this age of the "mad dash and quick hash," people's souls seem senselessly caught in an inextricable web of confusion and consternation. While technology affords humankind new luxuries and conveniences, human drought and desolation still persist as people seek a closer relationship with God. While the answers to humankind's material quests seem to be given through the achievements of science and new technology, questions of the heart and soul still linger as never before. Moreover, people appear sequestered and disillusioned by the amenities of society and are reclaiming those values inherent in the spiritual life. The pastor who utilizes the prophetic model must help to clarify the spiritual, social, and personal issues, pointing people back to the reality of God.

For example, one pastor related the difficulties he experienced in counseling a parishioner who had recently lost her husband. He spent long hours helping her through the bereavement process, but after ten one-hour sessions, he seemed to be making no progress. Finally, he thought that perhaps what this woman needed was not so much bereavement counseling as clarification that God still loved her. During the last year of his life, her husband had been placed in a nursing home. Subsequently, the wife incurred much guilt about this because she had come from a family where sick relatives were always taken in by other kin and almost never placed in nursing homes. She needed clarification that God still loved her despite that decision, which actually was best because the man had special needs she could not have provided. Hearing from her pastor that she was still loved by God, notwithstanding her actions, was essential to the woman's recovery of self-respect and personhood.[3]

Another example is the case of a recovering alcoholic. For years this man had running battles with his wife about buying her a red dress. He complained vehemently about having to "spend my hard-earned money to buy something you don't need!" The day after his wife died from cancer, he came to the funeral home with tears in his eyes and solemnly gave the director a beautifully wrapped box tied with a red bow. "Take this," he said to the director. "This is the red dress my wife always wanted but I was too cheap to buy for her. Please, sir, bury her in this dress."

The man, suffering guilt from this experience, spent long hours in counseling. His anguish was exacerbated by the fact that he had squandered thousands of dollars on alcohol, but didn't buy his wife "the only thing she ever asked for." Pastoral counseling needed to not only clarify for him the spiritual consequences of his actions, but also provide a redemptive way out of the guilt. The man had to be assured that despite his myopia and selfishness, he could still be the recipient of God's grace and love. Clarification of his actions, and the work of God notwithstanding, was indispensable in recovering a sense of self for this individual.[4]

The pastor as clarifier must be an ardent observer of the landscape of human personality and behavior. A good listener, he or she must decipher the cores of concern from which people relate their grief, anxiety, and the need to be valued as genuine persons of God.

Many people seek membership in the church out of a need to be clarified and confirmed humanly. There is something within human beings that desires to identify with a larger aggregate, for to be in community with others is to open the doors of human possibility and potential.

Moreover, the task of the prophetic pastor is to provide persons with the "spiritual blueprints and roadmaps" that will ultimately direct their paths back to the reality of God. Inasmuch as people restore themselves to that path, personal wholeness, healing, and realization of potential is actualized. The great tragedy of our times, observed one writer, is not that people ignore God, but that they live as though God does not really exist. There is a need today for rediscovery of the existence of God. It is essential to fathom ways in which that reality undergirds, empowers, and enamors human experience, in order to recover meaning, purpose, and vitality in life.

The pastor as clarifier is particularly significant in African American communities. No people, other than indigenous Americans, have undergone the ostracism, persecution, psychological abuse, and oppression of African Americans. No other group has experienced the perils and penalties of being defined and redefined by the larger culture. The effects of these machinations have created a devastating fallout in black households and communities throughout this nation.

Few groups have had as blatantly and ostensibly delineated for them the terms and conditions of nonacceptance; from the Three-fifths of a Man Doctrine to the practice of residential apartheid in segments of America today, the message of inferior status resonates clearly to many African Americans.

The pastor as clarifier must understand the particular needs of African American people. He or she must know something of the cultural matrix, the psychological and spiritual conditions under which many black Americans adversely labor. Knowledge of the social, political, and economic realities of American life help the pastor to discern the deeper underpinnings of the "American dilemma," allowing him to posit larger solutions to the various problems.

The prophetic model is even more apropos in considering these factors, for the pastor as prophet must have not only a sense of individual needs and pathologies, but an understanding of the larger context in which these problems emerge and impinge upon black life.

For example, pastors likely will discover that black churches have more sick and homebounds on their rolls than do other churches of similar size. This probability is not simply an affirmation that blacks suffer from more maladies and health complications than their white counterparts, but speaks to the larger social and cultural problems which depict the state of health in African American communities. Rather than distracting the pastor from the changes which will bring growth, these conditions can be recognized, addressed, and thus become a source of growth.

What social, political, and psychological factors adversely affect the health of African Americans? Besides having been acclimated to centuries of poor eating habits, and bad food which ultimately undermines health, other factors may well contribute to this phenomenon. The pastor as clarifier should have knowledge and acumen of how the larger issues and realities influence individual choices and decisions. Like the biblical prophets, she must discern how the collective social structures adversely impact the private lives of individuals.

For several years, residents of a New Jersey community had complained to authorities about the presence of malodorous and asphyxiating fumes. Nausea, dizziness, vomiting, and fainting were some of the resulting symptoms. Some initially attributed the problem to spoiled food sold by a neighborhood grocery. Others insisted that waste being dumped in a nearby vacant lot was the problem. One woman recalled, "I hear trucks late at night making all kinds of weird noises. They drop stuff off in dump trucks and drive off in a hurry."

An assembly of concerned residents went to the pastor for psychological counseling. The pastor thereupon recalled reading an article in a local newspaper about the specter of toxic dumping that was plaguing New Jersey residents. Only after extensive investigation by the pastor and others, was it discovered that a waste-removal company had released sludge into a nearby unauthorized dump site.[5]

That pastor had clarified the source of their problems and galvanized the resources to effectively address the critical issues. This is prophetic ministry in the social realm, although many personal issues with which these people struggled were directly attributed to this festering social ill. The pastor had to be astute enough to perceive this clandestine threat to the lives of community residents.

This particular incident and the pastor's leadership served as a launching point for a quantum leap in membership of his church. Because the pastor responded prophetically by clarifying an issue of ultimate concern to community residents, many people chose to unite with his congregation. By functioning as prophetic clarifier, he enhanced the church's community profile and subsequently drew new "sheep" into the flock.

The pastor also functions as a values clarifier. He assists people in *determining the parameters of spiritual and moral concern*. She helps to *clarify personal needs such as healing, direction, and methods of implementing positive spiritual change in people's lives*. As people face the "slings and arrows of outrageous fortune," the question often is "to be or not to be." People need direction, hope, the presence of one who will guide their steps and help restore confidence in God as they walk the trails of life.

It's not easy to function as clarifier in the lives of so many people. This requires an intimacy, a willingness to be and stay in touch with people in the areas of ultimate concern in their lives.

THE PASTOR AS CREATIVE CONFRONTER

The pastor must not only clarify but *creatively confront* the people and problems both he and they face. Often in discussing pastoral care, we avoid using the language of confrontation. It seems harsh, almost incongruous with the role of pastor as sympathizer and shepherd. Yet, if we are to seriously consider the elements of prophetic church growth, the pastor must exemplify courage in creatively confronting and addressing the serious problems that arise in the lives of parishioners and the church. God help the pastors who are afraid to take on the critical problems for fear of getting their clothing soiled and their hands dirty.

People today are seeking strong spiritual leadership. They want a leader who can firmly take problems on and help to bring about effective solutions. We stated earlier that a mark of biblical prophecy is a conviction with a prerequisite of courage. The pastor must show fortitude in the heat of battle and not shrink in tough times. He or she must find a way to be tough but tender, firm but flexible, confrontational but not abrasive.

One pastor recalled the necessity of creatively confronting a faithful member rumored to have been stealing money from the church. This person, also a money counter, was seen several times by other trustees slipping twenty-dollar bills into his pocket. This apparently went on for six months, but none of the other six counters ever accosted him with it. Finally, the pastor could no longer postpone the inevitable.[6]

In order to resolve the problem in a Christian manner, the pastor decided to follow the mandate in Matthew 18:15. He went to the man alone and confronted him with the facts. So incensed was the man that he vented his rage at the pastor, who fled in a storm. Resolutely determined to resolve the issue, the pastor took three of the counters with him to confront the man again, but the result was the same.

Because the man refused to meet with the pastor after a third request, the only recourse was to take the matter to the church. The man was summarily "expelled" from his duties as trustee but given a chance for a hearing, which he refused.

Furthermore, the pastor was faced with the added burden of confronting the trustees and counters who had observed what went on but chose to ignore it. As a result, some of them became angry at the pastor because, said one, they "weren't to blame."

The problem was resolved with the establishment of guidelines and policies which recommended a course of action if a member is suspected of stealing money from the church.

Creative confrontation of both the man and the counters, who were unwitting complicitors, was highly expedient, lest the church be torn asunder by potential conflict. The pastor needed to show courage even if it meant risking well-established relationships with certain people. Failure to act would have created a far greater problem, rending the church apart. Fortitude and aptitude were really required here.

People expect pastors to act on their moral authority, to address potential problems and demonstrate a will to resolve conflict, even if it means being seared by its fires. Countless churches have failed to grow simply because the pastoral leadership did not show courage, faith, and strength when the hour called for it. Creative confrontation is indispensable in dealing with the quagmires of human disparity and conflict.

Another experience had to do with a pastor whose great preaching brought in droves of new members each Sunday. However, once he preached them in, three of the older members ran them out. He brought them in one door and they were chased out the other. Finally, after observing this pattern for several months, he decided to confront the individuals with the facts.[7]

It was reported by a recent joinee that one of the three had said to him, "You can join this church if you want, but don't expect to serve in any leadership position because they're all filled by our older members." This statement completely offended the man, but instead of leaving the church, he decided to take the matter to the pastor. Apparently, statements of this type had been made to other prospective joiners, and the offensive words had prompted their complete defection. More than fifty members had been lost due to the mishandling of new members.

The hour came when the pastor and his lay leader had a meeting with the three persons. Instead of denying their actions, as had the man accused of stealing, they confessed them: "Yes, we discouraged participation in the church because we don't approve of all these new people coming in. Things were fine when we were small in membership. Now we hardly know the names of all these new people, and things are just not like they used to be."

"Well, why didn't you say something to me earlier about your discomfort? Why would you take your frustration out on the new members by discouraging participation in the church?" asked the pastor.

"We didn't *take out our frustration*. We just don't believe in having all these folks who are not going to work come into the church!"

"What makes you think they won't work, that there's no work to do? There's plenty of work for everyone here, don't you think? We have to give new members a chance, and this means the older members must be amenable to new people coming into the church. This helps everyone. The older members can't expect to be here forever. We must make room for new people," exclaimed the pastor.

While dialogue ensued from this creative confrontation, the pastor nonetheless was faced with the removal of the three individuals from their new-members-care positions. They were absolutely convinced that new people posed a threat to the existing church, and as long as they harbored this attitude, they would continue to "justifiably" push people out.

Absolving these persons of their duties after seeking redress to the problem created a storm of controversy in the church. The pastor was labeled "unfair, not a team player, one who did not conduct himself in a Christian manner."

A committee was formed to petition the district superintendent for a pastoral replacement. The pastor was castigated and branded as the central cause for disruption in the church. Neither relenting nor recanting his position, he firmly believed that creative confrontation was necessary to save the congregation from further strife. Had the three been allowed to continue their bent, the church would have died a slow and certain death.

Realizing what was at stake, some of the newer and many longstanding members rallied to the cause. The controversy was quelled and now the church enjoys phenomenal growth. A prophetic stance had to be taken. Conviction, investment, and vision—all were part of the pastor's rationale for taking a position. Creative confrontation of the wrongs and ills of the church, while not recommended by some, need to be implemented to save a congregation from demise.

This church, which happens to be United Methodist, avoided the fate of many United Methodist congregations, where the pastors beholden to an itinerant system are not invested in growth of the local church. In many cases of escalating conflict where members have placed a stranglehold on a church and thus killed it, the pastors have failed to confront the evil festering in their midst. As long as pastors are afraid to creatively confront these issues and conditions, the church cannot achieve its maximum growth potential.

Much of the resulting malaise and atrophy which cripples congregations has to do with the abuse of power by a few individuals. Failure to address these concerns often results in people who run their personal agendas at the expense of the church's public agenda, which is to save souls and win persons to Christ.

To confront creatively does not mean to use belligerent, bellicose, or ballistic tactics as a first course in dealing with problems in the parish. Creative confrontation means using the language of reconciliation and rapprochement as concerns are addressed and potential problems resolved. It does not advocate the use of "gunboat diplomacy" and "gangster logic" to eradicate the reality of evil in the church, but the manifestation of a firm volition in matters of great moral and ethical controversy, and a determination to steer the wrong to right. By courageously taking a stand against evil, the pastor as prophet exemplifies leadership which attracts those who seek a firm foundation for spiritual growth and leadership.

Frequently, conflict situations in the church are instigated by pastors who first utilize spiritual scare tactics and political intimidation to put people in line. Their methods are often abusive, abrasive, and ambivalent. They fail to explore more creative ways of handling conflict and are an integral part of the problem instead of the solution. The more austere methods of confrontation should be used only as a last resort, when all other avenues of resolution have failed and a church threatens to be destroyed. The first steps should be dialogue, in an attempt to find other ways of bridging the gaps of estrangement created by conflict situations.

One parishioner related frustration with his pastor because he always used "street tactics" to upbraid his congregation. This pastor went so far as to "curse people out" when they made some error or didn't follow through on an important assignment. While many people thought his approach refreshingly candid and sorely expedient in dealing with the "hard-headed negroes of his congregation," others abhorred it and left the church in protest. Confrontational, he certainly was. Creatively confrontational, he was not.[8]

THE PASTOR AS PROPHETIC RESTORER AND COMFORTER

The prophetic pastor must have not only a will to confront situations of evil and injustice, but an inclination to restore and comfort those in need of God's love and care. Jesus is often referred to as the great comforter. While he *confronted* the evil of his time, he also *comforted* the people as they struggled with their addictions, afflictions, and contradictions.

The image of pastor as comforter calls to mind the importance of the church in serving as a source of healing in our society. People are grieving in so many ways and are desperately seeking a balm, a refuge for their hurts, pains, alienation, and frustration. The church must provide solace for the brokenhearted and broken-spirited, the possessed and the dispossessed. The pastor as comforter accentuates the need for human-healing agencies in our times. The language of healing, listening, and caring is indispensable to the pastor in this role.

One minister delineated the importance of his role as comforter while serving a church in Chicago. "In many cases," he recalled, "people would simply come into my office and talk for an hour without my saying a word. They would finish, get up, and thank me for listening. I knew that by just hearing them, healing was taking place in their lives."[9]

Comforting often means demonstrating availability and a willingness to listen to the struggles and trials of a life experience.

Verbalizing is often not required, but presence and tenderness go a long way in helping people recover from their hurts, pain, and guilt.

In functioning within the three modes of prophetic pastoral care, it is essential that pastors understand when to use the appropriate response. It is highly problematic to confront a parishioner who needs to be comforted, or to comfort one who needs clarification or confrontation. There is a delicate balance in the use of these principles, and the pastor should take much care in studying each individual situation.

For example, we all know of people who have made serious mistakes. In an effort to purge themselves of guilt, they confess their wrongs. Perhaps they have been painfully victimized by their own transgressions, but being impervious to this, we immediately confront them by blaming them for what they've done. Needed here are not caustic, acrimonious reminders of their complicity in an act, but sympathy, compassion, and comfort as they struggle to come to terms with the consequences of their actions.

The biblical prophets understood that the comfort of God's people was the underlying objective of their mission and ministries. Isaiah 40:1-2a reminds us of a central task of the prophetic office: "Comfort, O comfort my people, says your God. Speak tenderly to Jerusalem." And Jeremiah poignantly asks, "Is there no balm in Gilead? Is there no physician there? Why then has the health of my poor people not been restored?" (8:22). One particularly heart-wrenching story was told by a pastor from Atlanta, Georgia:

> One day a woman came to the church asking to see me. My secretary invited her in and she sat down and immediately began crying and screaming at the top of her voice. After about five minutes of this, she regained her composure and began speaking in low, halting tones. "I need to talk with someone," she said. "I can't take it anymore!" "How can I help you?" I asked. She said, "My father has been making sexual advances toward my daughter."[10]

After conversing further, the minister discovered that the woman had been living with her birth father, who had also sired her three daughters. Now his perverted sickness had manifested itself in taking liberties with his granddaughter. Needless to say, the woman was devastated.

Further inquiry revealed that her birth mother had left the family because the father had taken sexual liberties with this daughter. Feeling helpless and powerless to resolve her dilemma, the daughter ended up in a common-law relationship with her father and finally sought help because of the sexual abuse of her child.

The pastor, hearing this story, was tempted to condemn and confront the woman for "being so base and mindless as to allow such iniquity to occur. Never in life had I experienced the indignation and medley of emotions I felt in hearing this woman's despair and grief."[11] Rather than blame the victim, which a more confrontational approach might have warranted, the minister sought to comfort this person whose life lay in ruins. Confrontation would have decimated the woman even more. Mercy, not judgment; grace, not condemnation, were sorely needed here.

In what ways can these principles of clarification, creative confrontation, and comfort be catalysts for church growth? In whatever way we assess the various rationale for the growth of black churches, one central factor in all this is the personality and profile of the pastor. While people are attracted to churches for a variety of reasons, the pastor who serves the congregation is crucial in church growth.

Without the pastor, whose vision, leadership, and style of ministry have much to do with whether a church grows or dies, the church lacks that cohesive element which rallies, empowers, and prepares the people of God for the church's present and future work. This does not mean that laity cannot be equally effective in expanding the church and developing it without pastoral leadership. It simply means that in the black church tradition, the pastor usually has a vital role in this process. Without the pastor, a church can find itself caught in the *theology of drift,* or without the navigator necessary to steer it to port.

Why is the role of the minister so essential to the growth of the African American church? First—and this may work to either the benefit or the detriment of black people—is the dependence upon a messianic and prophetic style of leadership. Since the days of slavery, blacks have viewed their emancipation in terms of the biblical paradigm of the leader who liberates the masses of oppressed. Moses' leading of the Hebrew children from Egypt into the Promised Land is one example. The leadership model of Jesus, as one man who effects the salvation of the entire human race, is another. We can also see contemporary examples of the messianic leadership style—from Marcus Garvey to Martin Luther King, Jr., and Malcolm X.[12]

Black people have always looked to the pastor as the unifying, galvanizing force of the African American community, and to the black church as the bulwark of its social and political concerns.

Second, the personality, dynamism, and charisma of the pastor as a person are very important in achieving successful growth of the black church, for he or she must boldly and intrepidly espouse truth, demonstrate strength and tenacity in articulating the concerns of black people, and have a capacity to assuage their ills and hurts.

Inasmuch as the pastor clarifies and confronts the status quo, calling into accountability the powers and principalities, he or she discloses a special calling which clearly distinguishes that person from the masses. Without him, their deepest concerns could not be voiced. Without her cry in the wilderness, the people have no advocate for the perils that plague them.

Because courage and a willingness to tell both white and black folks the truth is so highly valued in the African American community, the pastor's representative embodiment of these ideals on its behalf summons the consolidation of its interests and power. These personality factors are key in building viable churches. The people seek leaders who will sincerely and unselfishly enunciate the true claims of their community and point them toward the referents of empowerment that will accomplish their aims. If a pastor can achieve these objectives, credibility and reliability become the hallmarks of her personality and reputation. Such gifts go far in winning the lost and wayward to Christ.

Third, and institutionally speaking, the African American church is still the most significant bastion of leadership, creativity, and power in the African American community. No other constellation of power exists which so influences the thinking, values, and ethical codes of black people in America. The black church has always been the source of social consciousness, political enfranchisement, and the incorporation of economic interests, and the black pastor's role has been fundamental in the leadership process.

While much of the data disclosed in this chapter focus upon the interior dimensions of the church's prophetic ministry, these same principles can be applied in the social arena. That is, the pastor in his role may be creatively confrontational relative to the powers and principalities within the church, but can be equally creative in confronting those social and political powers in the larger society. The pastor who demonstrates courage and boldness in the social arena is likely to attract a following interested in addressing such issues. Therefore, prophetic ministry in a social context can also effect positive church growth.

Clarification, creative confrontation, and *comfort* are the three principles of prophetic pastoral care which can be applied both within the church and in the larger society. They are principles that require sensitivity, acumen, and a willingness to apply them as useful means of implementing church growth. The pastor must be unafraid to confront existing evil, clarify for people the core concerns of their lives, and help them develop the resources to solve their problems. She must be able to comfort them as they seek redemptive solutions to their problems and pain, by demonstrating empathy and sympathy toward issues of ultimate concern.

CHECKLIST AND SUMMARY
OF PROPHETIC PASTORAL-CARE PRINCIPLES

Clarification Checklist

The pastor must continually evaluate the way he or she relates to people through pastoral care.

_____A. Does your pastoral-care style help people to clarify the critical issues of their lives?

_____B. In listening to people, are you really able to hear them from the center of their spiritual concerns and provide clarity about the issues they're facing?

_____C. Do you have a sense of the sacred, and can you delineate it for those who are seeking greater spiritual clarity?

___D. Are you familiar with the vast welter of human concerns which impact individuals in various ways and point to these sources in helping people to clarify these issues?

Creative Confrontation Checklist

Do not be afraid to creatively confront people during the course of your ministry. What is your current style of confrontation?

___A. Do you exercise the three B's—belligerence, ballistics, and bellicosity—as a first resort in solving conflict?

___B. Or do you exercise the three C's—caring, comfort, and compassion?

___C. Periodically, evaluate your style of confrontation. Do you use the language of caring and reconciliation, or are you quick to chastize and reprimand for mistakes?

Restoration/Comfort Checklist

___A. What modes of comfort do you extend to those who need pastoral care?

___B. What comfort skills have you cultivated in dealing with the people of God?

___C. How do you extend comfort to those who have personally estranged themselves from you?

___D. What counseling techniques do you apply to people with various types of grief?

CHAPTER FIVE

Three Principles
of Prophetic Education

W hile prophetic worship services and pastoral care are essential in growth of the black church, Christian education is equally vital as the church moves toward the twenty-first century. Black people today seek a church that not only inspires and uplifts the human spirit but one that challenges the mind through sound educational programs and good Christian teaching.

The basic tasks of the educational ministry in the growing prophetic church are to raise critical consciousness, help people develop a pragmatic and viable faith, and assist them in the acquisition of spiritual principles, through the development and implementation of meaningful programs. Three basic principles are important here: *investigation, interpretation,* and *application.* The educational ministry of the prophetic black church must exhort persons to investigate, interpret, and apply the central truths and claims of the gospel.

INVESTIGATION

One of the basic problems that has crippled the black church in the past is the climate of repression which teaches people to *not* investigate, challenge, or critically appraise the Scriptures or other religious tenets. People are often told not to question what they read or hear regarding the interpretation of God's Word. The ministerial style is often autocratic and authoritarian, and brooks no opposition to open inquiry. Such an educational environment is cultivated in an atmosphere of fear, reprisals, and superstitions often bordering on the fanatical. The pastor is invariably the final word on all matters, even if his or her interpretation is skewed and specious.

A prophetic educational program designed to help churches grow must be *meaningful, relevant, and open to the needs and aspirations of God's people.* It must cultivate a spirit of investigation and inquiry which embraces and challenges certain traditions and creates a context for raising critical consciousness. Openness to inquiry is essential here, for people today in the black church, like their peers in the white church, are seeking new, fresh interpretations that will unearth truth for their lives as they struggle with the deeper meanings of God's Word.

The prophetic educational program encourages not only the open investigation of God's Word, but the unrestricted access to the experience of life itself. All Christians should be avid investigators of life, ranging from things spiritual to matters economic and political.

The prophetic Christian is concerned with all of life, as Jesus' ministry so clearly instructs—the social and political, the material and spiritual. Anything that has to do with investigating, interpreting, and understanding, that will enhance and augment life in all its myriad forms and possibilities, should be the prophetic objective of Christian education.

Biblical Inquiry

For example, in developing a Bible-study class, the participants should be encouraged to explore background information on the Bible and the development of certain scriptural texts. They should be challenged to ferret out the geographical, political, and commercial climate of specific Bible chronologies. Bible study should not be an exercise in interpretive tyranny, where one explanation suffices and supplants all others.

Challenge people to investigate the history of Scripture and the relevancy of certain passages for today. Exhort them to study the text and context of specific biblical and contemporary situations. *Investigate, investigate, investigate*—this should be the epithet of all religious inquiry! The mood, the circumstances of the texts, the phrasing, the author, the audience, the theme of the text—all these should be investigated by those seeking a better understanding of the Word of God.

African Influences
in the Judeo-Christian Heritage

Another important element in a viable educational program, of particular interest to a rising number of blacks, is the history and role of black people in the development of the Scriptures. Much of the Old Testament speaks of Egypt, which is in Africa. How much African influence do we see in the formation of Hebrew and current Middle Eastern culture? White racism has done much to obliterate or negate black people's role in the formation of biblical history and culture. Prophetic education in the black church will encourage the investigation of such valuable knowledge and information, as a basis for illuminating black people's understanding of their vital role in the early development of the Judeo-Christian heritage.

Other concerns around the African basis of Christianity have to do with the Ten Commandments, which are curiously reminiscent of portions of the Egyptian negative confessions. Temple practices and rituals of the later Hebraic or Israelite traditions bear striking resemblance to Egyptian temple ceremonies. Also, the idea of the Holy Spirit and the notion of a crucified Savior smack of African influences. Jesus himself was recorded by the historian Josephus as being "melangrous," or blackskinned. How could the Hebrew children spend more than four hundred years in Africa and not have been influenced by its culture and people?[1]

The educational program of the prophetic black church should inspire constructive, responsible inquiry into the role of African peoples in the development and dissemination of the Judeo-Christian traditions. Developing an educational program which is primarily Afrocentric in focus will help to establish the church as a place of serious inquiry. Such an image of the African American church is much needed by those of the younger generation, who, in contrast to their forebears, believe in questioning the data and challenging the central propositions of the Christian faith.

While many individuals in both black and white communities disparage the notion of Afrocentric inquiry, I believe that the information such inquiry discloses is extremely valuable in establishing the black church as a center of truth in society. How can a church that is not proud of its heritage continue to grow?

The African American church has often been criticized by the more radical segments of the black community as being a major contributor to the enslavement and oppression of black people in America. Much of this problem can be ascribed to the Eurocentric nature of Christian teachings, the interpretations of which contain a white racist and colonial slant. It has been argued that Christianity was utilized by white colonial powerbrokers to pacify indigenous peoples, as a prelude to their subsequent colonization and annihilation. Thus, many black radicals have dubbed Christianity the "white man's religion."

While it is true that the Christian religion was used as a tool in the subjugation and enslavement of nonwhite races in the world, its foundations were influenced by black Africans, and its teachings originally were of a liberating character. The original "followers of the Way," as they were called, were part of a faith-and-freedom movement which initially put them at odds with the ruling powers and authorities. In fact, one might say that the Christian-faith movement has been the longest sustained revolution in the history of humankind. No other religious or political revolution has perpetuated itself for so long.

While it is true that the black church contains conservative elements which support uncritically the existing order, it also has been on the cutting edge of significant revolutionary change. The recent Civil Rights and Black Power movements attest to the positive influence of the African American church as catalyst for constructive change in American society.

Biblically speaking, the prophet was a significant source of education for the people of God. He either redirected their attention to the authentic roots of their spiritual and cultural traditions, or raised their consciousness of how the precepts of those customs made iniquity, apostasy, and oppression intolerable in the eyes of God. The prophet thus helped to transform the awareness of God's people by revealing the critical claims of their faith, claims long negated and obviated by an abandonment of the terms of the covenant.

In other words, the prophet reclaimed those vital elements of the spiritual tradition which serve as a source of empowerment for the people of God. By exhorting and admonishing a return to the spiritual and historical foundations of the faith, the prophet served as the herald of, according to Brueggeman, the "alternative consciousness," which is essential in transforming one's spiritual and existential situation. The prophetic African American church must similarly advocate a return to the authentic sources and traditions of Scripture by revealing its African influences— or it cannot grow responsibly.

Black people are diligently seeking the truth: the truth about their past history; their role and influence in the development of world civilizations, religions, and culture; and the truth about how such vestiges have been extirpated from world-history books. Since religion remains one of the most dynamic sources of vitality in African American communities, it should encourage and facilitate the investigation of the truth of black people's role in the development of the Judeo-Christian traditions.

One pastor who desired to raise the consciousness of parishioners about blacks in the Bible was met with such forceful opposition that it threatened to destroy the church. He commented, "All I wanted to do was share some of the findings of my own research, which I thought would be welcomed by church members." He recalled hearing such comments as, "We don't want to hear all that black stuff," and "Next you'll be telling us that Jesus was black!"

People essentially did not want to hear the truth, for they had been brainwashed into believing that black people had had no positive influence on the development of Christianity. Information that could have been investigated in a spirit of openness and freedom was rejected through fear of discovering a truth too painful to bear. The pastor left that church for a progressive congregation more amenable to his creative ideas.[2]

In reestablishing itself as the vital dispenser of knowledge and the trumpeter of truth in American society, the African American church must develop prophetic educational programs which speak to the historical and contemporary truths of black contributions to Judeo-Christian traditions and world civilization. The more such truths are disseminated, the more readily blacks are able to envision themselves as positive transformers of life and society, rather than passive recipients of reality.

The prophetic black church should train people for critical reflection and inquiry, to disclose those truths which vitally reconnect blacks to their active, transformative role in human history, and thus to the present society. Such pursuits help to raise consciousness, to establish and apply a pragmatic and viable faith which will facilitate the translation of the old order into the new.

Existential Inquiry

No areas of concern are off limits to prophetic Christian inquiry. Contemporary reality, in all its forms and possibilities, must be explored with equal fervor and zeal. The task of prophetic education, in an existential sense, is to critically investigate the norms, forms, and possibilities of life in the present context. How can the church become a viable forum for the exploration of new vistas and ideals for positive change?

The church need not be the repository of creative social change, but it can act as an impetus for such change. Instead of invariably following the lead of society, the church can function as its visionary leader by disclosing new truths and directing people to the ultimate ground of their spiritual and existential concerns, which inevitably lead to positive transformation.

For example, instead of functioning in a *world maintaining* mode, the church can function *world historically* by espousing principles and ideals which help to actualize the bases for establishment of positive social change.[3] Rather than function in a relationship of economic dependency with society and even with its own parishioners, the church would undertake viable economic projects which would refurbish communities and capitalize on the hidden resources and strengths of communities and parishioners.

Seldom is the church conceived as a viable economic center for community development. However, a visionary world-historical approach could catapult the church into such an arena. For this to transpire, a spirit of openness to new ideas, through the free exploration of existential possibilities within the church, must be nurtured. A magnanimous spirit of inquiry may well mean the reconfiguration of the church's role in society, which would establish new models and paradigms of ecclesiastical functioning.

Why can't the church revision itself as a viable vehicle for economic revitalization in African American communities? Conventional orthodoxy represses a spirit of investigation, which means that such ventures never come to fruition. Adopting the seven last words—"We never did it that way before"—does not help to promote such ideals.

Needed is an entrepreneurial spirit for new modes of inquiry, with the subsequent repositioning of the African American church as a viable leader in the redevelopment of black communities in America. This may well mean positing the African American church as a bastion of economic and educational opportunities, which will effect and sustain the long-term transformation of society.

Such an approach is surely prophetic, in that it anticipates the future and calls for responsible preparation. The prophet calls the people to prepare for the coming reign of God's Kingdom, a reign that is present, but not yet realized. The prophetic church helps to pave the way for the actualization of the Kingdom of God in human history by establishing educational programs that will foster such change.

Existential inquiry demands the opening of new windows of social, political, and religious consciousness, and proposes other ways of bridging the existential with spiritual concerns, for the benefit of black people as well as the larger society.

The ministry of Jesus provides the rationale and norms for such creative exploration. Jesus' concern is for the whole of humanity— its spiritual, economic, social, and political welfare. It is provincial to devise programs or ministries that simply speak to the Spirit without considering the entire spectrum of social concerns which impoverish and debase the human spirit.

In urban black communities in the central cities, the prophetic role of the African American church in addressing these concerns is particularly vital. Blight, despondency, and existential despair often characterize life in the cities as many communities, seemingly under siege, are deluged with drugs, poverty, unemployment, and crime. The African American church must raise a prophetic voice in the midst of these concerns and make constructive proposals for positive transformation.

The Sunday Sermon

We stated in the chapter on prophetic worship that part of the appeal of worship is the presentation of an inspirational and informative sermon. Equally important is that the sermon evidence a concern for life in the larger community and demonstrate the pastor's capacity for critical inquiry.

Gone are the days when preachers can simply "moan and groan" in the pulpit without providing substantive information and knowledge for the congregation. The modern black churchgoer is seeking inspiration and information, sermonic form and content. There should be something of educational value in the Sunday sermon which excites the imagination and encourages the pursuit of more information.

The Sunday sermon should therefore have something of educational value in it and demonstrate the pastor's penchant for diligent preparation and careful exposition of ideas. I am not suggesting that sermons become exercises in pedantic erudition, pretentious, pompous, and ostentatious. Some sermons are so "scholarly," they fail to reach the audience.

I am advocating the diligent and faithful study of God's Word and the development of sermons which challenge the minds and hearts of God's people without violating their sensibilities or the integrity of scriptural texts. Pastors should discover something of value in the course of their studies that sheds new light on both the texts of Scripture and the context of people's lives.

The Sunday sermon is a source of appeal for potential members, for it is one of the few ways people can gauge the intellectual and spiritual profile of a particular congregation. The pastor should be adept at drawing upon the folk traditions of black culture, as well as at explicating the relevancy of science and technology for black life today. People are seeking new ideas and vistas, creative frontiers of intellectual and spiritual discovery, which challenge and inspire them. The Sunday sermon should, at least periodically, provide a glimpse into new gateways of knowledge and understanding.

Many younger black men have stereotyped notions of the black preacher and the black church. They imagine an overweight, finger-licking, chicken-eating, Cadillac-driving, womanizing, money-grubbing, silk-suit-wearing, uneducated preacher against the backdrop of a naively exploitable congregation. This antediluvian portrait still looms large in the minds of many male blacks who have dismissed the preacher and church altogether as frivolous, unstudied, and impertinent.

As pastors become more educated, this archaic image can be dispelled from the minds of the younger generations of blacks. I am not saying that the "whoop" and "moan" so characteristic of some black preaching styles be abandoned altogether or that folk images and traditions be relinquished. This is a unique aspect of our religious heritage and should be preserved, as Henry Mitchell also has urged.[4] I am saying that along with that "hoop," there should abound substance which provides knowledge that will lead to the progressive empowerment and spiritual transformation of African American people. The dispensation of vital information and knowledge, based upon critical and responsible investigative scholarship as evidenced in the Sunday sermon, is essential.

Preaching and teaching should be accentuated in the Sunday sermon. Preaching inspires. Teaching informs. Both the heads and the hearts of parishioners should be reached through these idioms.

INTERPRETATION

The issue of interpretation discloses the need for developing a hermeneutic which supports the goals of prophetic black church growth. It means revisiting and possibly revising the definitions, concepts, paradigms, and interpretive schema which inform the practice of ministry within the black church. Much of the way the church prophetically grows depends upon the modes of analyses by which the church envisions, defines, and interprets its mission and ministry. If the church simply views itself as the upholder of the status quo and not the precursor of spiritual and social transformation, this image will be informed in part by the parameters by which it has defined itself. This assumption about the link between social transformation and growth is precisely opposite from what is claimed to work in the growth of a white church.

The modes and principles of interpretation are critical in developing a prophetic educational program. They shape vision, clarify concepts, and point actually and symbolically to the realities the church seeks to empower and change. How does the church interpret its mission and ministry? What ecclesial models are employed which help the church configure itself in the community it serves? Avery Dulles' *Models of the Church* is helpful here.[5]

Innovation

A great problem today is the church's presupposition that the models utilized to define itself are already given. Invariably, in speaking of the "Church," we conceptualize a specific structure of organization and operation. Yet, the standard orthodoxies of interpretation utilized to define church structure may not coincide with the particular mission and goals of the prophetic black church.

For example, the alternative model may not have the traditional boards and committees which normally deploy the church's mission. It may contain a conglomeration of other entities which are more capable of effecting the prophetic mission. Such alternative structures may also better lend themselves to positive growth in membership.

A prophetic educational program which values the development of various modes of interpretation will encourage the creative innovation of new ideas which transcend traditional ecclesial constructs.

Rites of Passage Programs and Black Cultural Institutes

One particular concept developed by the educational ministry of our church through the auspices of the Imani Institute is a Rites of Passage program.[6] There is nothing within the orthodox church structures which creates a precedent for the development of this innovative idea. The cultivation of the program, along with the black cultural institute, is based upon the current needs of urban black youth and the desire to promote positive mentoring relationships with them.

Numerous black congregations in the Detroit metropolitan area have started such programs. Fellowship Chapel, under the leadership of Wendell Anthony; the Hartford Memorial Baptist Church, under Charles G. Adams; and our own Imani Institute, are a few. Such programs are designed to equip black youth with the spiritual, cultural, and material resources which will help them envision themselves as agents of positive change in their communities and in the larger society.

Other programs, such as the Frederick Douglass Lecture series and the Black Cultural Arts Festival offered during African American History month, are innovative projects developed through the educational program of Hope Church which celebrate the life cultures and global legacies of black people from the African diaspora.

Innovative programs of this type must be encouraged by a spirit of creative inquiry and investigation, an openness to new concepts and paradigms of ministry.

Holistic Spirituality

Another program, the Spiritual Life Center, has been inspired by the spirit of creative interpretation and innovation at Hope Church. While this ministry does not explicitly address the political and social concerns of African Americans, it nevertheless provides an educational resource which will facilitate positive spiritual growth within that community.

The purpose of this educational ministry, conceived out of a prophetic concern for the health and wholeness of the people of God in African American communities, is to educate people in the area of fasting, nutrition, and holistic spirituality.

The Spiritual Life Center bridges concepts of Eastern and

Western spiritual enlightenment by offering seminars and classes on yoga, meditation, and other disciplines. An equally innovative program developed under the aegis of this center provides instruction on stress reduction, healing and wholeness, marital enrichment, and adolescent parenting.

Human spirituality is concerned with both body and mind, but Western paradigms largely ignore the importance of the former. Few existing ecclesiologies embrace the synthesis of Eastern and Western models, where tending the spirit is intimately balanced with nurturing the body and mind with the proper exercise and nutrition. This is of critical concern in African American communities where poor health is rampant, and in African American churches where cakes, pies, and good soul food are an integral part of the weekly fellowship. One colleague amusingly stated that the church that eats together stays together, and this always has been part of the unique character of the black church.

While fellowship in African American communities revolves around the hearty and festive celebrations of "breaking bread and eating until one's heart is content," a great need exists for holistic spirituality and nutritional counseling within the black church. Emphases here should be on adopting those health and dietary practices which promote optimum spirituality and longevity. The Scriptures exhort us to be good stewards of the body, as well as of the mind.

Prophetic education institutes programs which help to establish holistic spirituality as a ministerial practice. The development of such creative ministries will largely depend upon the principles of interpretation which create a context for the implementation of innovative ideas. Simply following traditional equations and formulas of the way a church is to be structured and operated may not suffice to meet the ultimate needs of a particular community. Risk-taking and the daring to do something new are hallmarks of innovative churches.

Redefining Jazz as Sacred Music

This spirit of creativity and interpretation may be explored also in other areas of the church. For example, I have long held the belief that jazz, known as American classical music, should be incorporated into the worship format of black churches. A good place to begin is during the offertory. Many people who have conventional and conservative notions of church tradition and ritual would find such ideas repulsive. Jazz, they insist, is not sacred music and clearly falls outside the parameters of religion.

The problem is one of defining and redefining: What is *sacred*? And this is essentially a matter of interpretation. For too long, black people have permitted racist whites and reactionary blacks to define and valuate the sacred in black life.

When jazz first burst upon the American scene and showcased in brothels and other dubious nocturnal environs because it could not be played in more conventional settings, it acquired the label "devil's music." The people who stigmatized it were confusing the music itself with the milieu in which it was played.[7]

The problem is similar to the one created by the Wesleys when they adapted Christian lyrics to bar tunes. Jazz played in Peking makes it no more Chinese than a bordello makes it devil's music. It's one thing to categorize something as fiendish if it incessantly brings out the worst in people. It's quite another to besmirch it by virtue of association, and that's what certain people did to the only authentically indigenous art form that America has ever given the world, which may have prevented its subsequent inclusion in the music repertoire of black churches.

Classical is defined as "something which transcends its origins," and American classical music has certainly done this the world over. The people who have thus defined and discredited it don't understand that the music itself originally evolved out of the sacred traditions of the African American church. Many of the earliest exponents of jazz received their musical training in the black church. If the gospel music of Thomas Dorsey is sacred, then why not the "sheets of sound" of John Coltrane? Both evolve from the sacred canons of African American culture and life.

The incorporation of jazz into the worship traditions of the prophetic black church is indeed a daringly innovative idea, for its acceptance would require a reorientation and revaluation of thinking on behalf of God's people. The greatest obstacle to such change might be African Americans themselves, since their religious pedestrianism often thwarts the exploration of new thoroughfares. Often, in celebrating the more precocious black church, we seldom lament the staunch, entrenched orthodoxies of those "nonprogressive" churches which stifle the growth and development of African American communities.

Innovation may be propositional or oppositional. It need not take such radical expression as the incorporation of jazz into the musical repertoire of black churches. It may simply mean transforming the existing repertoire from the flat, dull, and unimaginative to the wholly creative, inspirational, and inventive. While the inclusion of jazz for some may be an oppositional extreme, the altering of existing canons of gospels, spirituals, and classics to more creative arrangements may be less threatening to the congregation, thereby achieving similar positive results. This also can occur in other areas of the church's ministry.

Countless numbers of unchurched blacks who are looking to unite with more progressive congregations would gladly support such churches if their ministries evinced some inclination toward positive growth and change. They too are looking toward celebrating the established traditions and norms of black church life, such as inspirational worship services, fellowship, and activism in the community. But they equally desire programs which challenge their thinking and empower spiritual growth and progressive social transformation. They want a new church, a prophetic church which unapologetically observes black life and culture, and stresses the value of education.

Evaluation

One of the crucial strategies in developing the Spiritual Life Center at Hope United Methodist Church was the distribution of a needs survey. By polling the congregation, the people's readiness to support such a venture could be appraised. Congregational endorsement of new programs have much to do with whether the people perceive that real needs are being met by them. Accordingly, *where there is no interest, the programs perish.*

One pastor related frustration in developing a ministry she believed the church badly needed, but only a modicum of evaluation was done to determine whether the church would really support it. Without selling the concept and assessing congregational needs, she presented her monumental program to the executive board. Needless to say, the idea, which happened to be a great one, died at that board meeting. A ship that had all the promise of sailing the high seas never left port because of inadequate preparation and evaluation.

This same pastor took the same idea to another parish. There she assessed the needs, conditions, and readiness of the church to buy into it. Winning their approval, the program now enjoys astounding success and has contributed significantly to the growth of the church. The achievement of her efforts was also strengthened by the support of the larger community, which saw the need for establishing such a program. While a day-care center is not exactly a revolutionary concept, it has proved an invaluable tool in the growth of her church.[8] Again, education without evaluation is like a house without foundation. Evaluation is thus an essential principle in establishing and perpetuating viable educational programs for prophetic church growth.

APPLICATION

The final principle of prophetic education is the *practical application of knowledge and information.* The concept and precepts of prophetic education must be not only conceived but pragmatically applied. The church is good at telling people *what to do,* but often short on telling them *how to do it.*

In order to increase the growth of the black church through prophetic educational principles, educators must also have an understanding of the structure and methods of prophetic motifs. If a primary objective of prophetic education is the personal and social transformation of individuals and society, *what are the specific principles, and how can they be applied in the African American context?* It is essential to have a broad understanding of Christian beliefs. It is imperative to understand and simplify the prophetic principles.

In this configuration process, some thought must be given to the *how* of this process. The *how* will depend largely upon the *what,* and the *what* is predicated upon the *who.* People not only must be encouraged to think differently, creatively, but must have some understanding of how such thinking can be duplicated and applied in the church and community.

In desiring to increase the membership of the church through a prophetic educational ministry, one must first understand that a basic premise of African American culture is the need for ongoing, positive change which can meliorate one's spiritual, material, and social conditions. The church must, therefore, not only embody the principles of change through its own innovative programming, but impart knowledge about how the creative thinking which brought about these programs can be applied in the personal realm. The prospects of offering this type of educational ministry will incite curiosity and attract black people to the church, since the need for constructive alternatives are already presupposed within the larger culture.

For example, in developing our Rites of Passage program, which is both creative and innovative, we understood that black youth in urban areas is at high risk for suicide, homicide, and fratricide. The specter of crime, drugs, and disillusionment which envelopes the black community has taken a horrendous toll. The church prophetically responded to the problem by developing an educational program that encourages them to think about the way they think and helps them begin to re-envision those positive alternatives which, when practically applied, can effect personal change. The creative incentives which inspired the development of the program are the same catalysts which, when instilled in our youths, can change their thinking.

Teaching the application of transformative knowledge to people provides them with the wherewithal to act as subjects of change, not objects whimsically and woefully manipulated by other beings and powers in their environment.

Prophetically increasing church membership also can mean helping people apply biblical principles through the teachings of Jesus. People are hungry for new ways to apply biblical knowledge. How can one develop an understanding of the methods by which the precepts of the faith can be lived? What are the principles of fasting, and how can they be actualized? How does one resist evil in daily experiences with co-workers, family, even members of the church? How can the precepts of faith be developed to achieve a closer relationship with God?

Prophetic education seeks to answer such questions so that the *practice of faith* is as real and instinctive as breathing.

But the development of application is a painstaking and piecemeal process. Too much of Christian preachment belies the real struggle involved in attaining the principles of faith. Many people falsely assume that their lives will be briskly transformed through some supernatural occurrence, like a bolt of lightning striking them, or a still small voice whispering to them at an NBA championship game. Not that God cannot transform lives in such a manner, but the expectation of a sudden transfiguration in consciousness without expending the labor required to attain these practical spiritual principles often confuses people about the real trials involved in transforming spiritual awareness.

The prophetic church seeks to clarify the real conditions for acquisition and application of the spiritual knowledge that leads to personal and social transformation. It is not enough to simply exhort people *what to do* without providing a blueprint of *how to do it*. If people need to transform their lives for the better, how can they achieve this goal through the application of biblical knowledge? If an aggregate of people desire to improve the quality of life in their community, how can they utilize Christian principles to achieve these aims?

If a coterie of residents came to the church to solicit assistance in ridding their community of drug dealers, what would be the response? "Turn the other cheek? Pray about it until a change comes? Trust in the Lord always and wait on Him? Resist not evil? Blessed are the patient, for they will get results? Render unto drug dealers the things that are drug dealers'?"

The application for prophetic prescripts do not advocate backing down from such challenges, any more than the prophet would abandon the dangerous task of calling into accountability the despots and tyrants or Jesus would shun bearing his cross. The concern is for the feasible, viable, practical application of knowledge that will bring about positive transformation of both individuals and communities. Prophetic education for church growth thereby accentuates the necessity of acquiring such information and its concomitant values and precepts.

Investigation, interpretation, and application are just three principles of prophetic education that can lead to church growth. The black church today, in calling people to Christ, must embody and reflect the respect for knowledge and information characteristic of the larger culture and society. Daniel Bell, Anthony Giddens, and others have delineated the power centers of knowledge, information, and technology which pivotally determine the future of society. Such are the axis entities that may well determine our future.[9]

The prophetic black church can ill afford to be simply a repository of information, but must, if you will, be a *transformatory* of the values, knowledge, and information which impact the future of black people in America.

CHECKLIST AND SUMMARY
OF PROPHETIC EDUCATION PRINCIPLES

Investigation Checklist

___A. What kind of educational program currently exists in your church? Does the existing program encourage critical and creative thinking about Scripture and the Christian faith?

___B. What kind of investigative ethos has been established in your educational programs? Do your programs encourage the careful pursuit of knowledge and information, or is the current climate one of entrenched orthodoxy, accentuated by the repression of new and creative ideas?

Interpretation Checklist

___A. How much latitude for innovation is provided by your current ministries?

___B. When did you last develop an educational program designed to meet the particular needs of the congregation you now serve? How much of your existing program is specifically designed to meet the unique needs of African American populations?

___C. What modes of interpretation do you encourage in your educational ministry?

Application Checklist

___A. Does your current educational program underscore "how to" faith principles?

___B. How much of your existing program is designed to help people clarify the practice of Christian principles?

Three Principles
of Prophetic Evangelism

T he recent proliferation of literature on evangelism as a tool for church growth attests to its importance. Few churches today have instituted prophetic evangelism programs designed to bring persons to Christ. In fact, a major criticism of the church has been its laid-back approach to bringing new persons into its fold. We live in an age when evangelism committees don't invite people to church and don't have systematic visitation programs to tell people the Good News of the gospel.

In the prophetic church, to invite is not enough. The church must offer something of value which inspires people to stay, once invited and there. Too often people come in one door and go out another because the church has failed to develop programs for membership nurture and care after admission to membership. Three principles are essential to prophetic evangelism and will help churches grow:

1. *Proclamation* of the Good News
2. *Propagation* and communication of the message
3. *Participation* open to all.

PROCLAMATION

Proclamation is the process of conveying something to people not through words alone, but also through actions. An older preacher once commented to me that the greatest sermon I would ever preach would not be with words, but with the way I lived. The old adage, "Actions speak louder than words," is true even in the prophetic church.

Proclamation is an important aspect of prophetic evangelism, for it is the "show and tell" of church growth. In an age when leaders don't mean what they say or say what they mean, when religious leadership and the church are undergoing crises in moral authority, people are searching for the truth, not half-truths, and for leadership that will tell it like it really is.

The church has experienced a paradoxical relationship with many of the disillusioned and unchurched. On one hand, the church utilizes the language of caring and invitation. It postures hospitality to the public by claiming to be open to everyone, without regard to race, ethnicity, or national origin. It proclaims an open door policy to any and all who would come: "Whosoever will, let him come."

Yet, in thinking about the churches with which we've had personal experience, we usually find only closed doors. What we painfully discover is a "country-club" attitude, an "only for the initiated" mentality, which doesn't really stand for what it professes. For this reason many people consider the church highly hypocritical. It says one thing but actually does another. It proclaims that all are children of God, worthy of God's grace as long as "they look and act like us." The same deception and duplicity characteristic of the larger society has infested the church, and many people are highly irritated by it.[1]

Thousands of would-be church members have this perspective, yet are not so opposed that they can't be converted to a new attitude. Winning them to Christ will have as much to do with the attitude the church proclaims that it manifests in backing up what it professes. The church must make concerted and persistent efforts to be consistent in practicing what it preaches.

Proclamation is the process of announcing something. In the case of Christianity, the church proclaims the Good News of the Risen Christ, one who vanquishes evil and death through the resurrection. This victorious attitude is bequeathed to those who possess and profess faith in him, and it is open to those who freely and joyfully follow him. But more than lip service, it requires principled and action-oriented behavior.

The prophetic church calls persons back to God through the proclamation of God's Word. That proclamation is an announcement buttressed by firm belief and consistent corresponding action—on behalf of believers, for unbelievers. Yet it is not so esoteric that all cannot partake of its fullness and glory. *Proclamation is calling people back to God through words and actions. It is inviting and keeping people in the household of faith.*

Interpersonal Relationships

Those who come to the prophetic church must *feel* that it is *living out* its Good News proclamations. The greatest evangelical tool for building viable churches is the creation of a spirit of acceptance, love, and respect generated through interpersonal relationships among members and nonmembers. If the church is full of back-biting, name calling, vehemence and vindictiveness, people will seldom unite. If, on the other hand, people sense that the church is a place of positive affirmation, caring, and fellowship for all, it is highly possible that people will choose to belong to it.

Both *members and nonmembers* gain a sense of belonging through genuine sharing and caring. A major deterrent to church growth is the exclusion of nonmembers from participation in the life of the church. If the church proclaims openness, hospitality, and fellowship to all, as Christ's Word demands, this should include members and nonmembers, churched and unchurched, saved and unsaved.[2]

Too often the church excludes people from its fellowship and membership circles by immediately throwing up membership smoke screens and other hurdles which keep people out rather than inviting them in. The church's attitude and position on such matters is communicated most often through interpersonal relationships. If a climate of hostility exists among members toward nonmembers, the church will never experience viable growth because it cuts people off from a feeling of belonging. No one wants to unite with a church where petty hostilities and aspersions are cast toward members or nonmembers.

The way people relate to one another, whether issues of ultimate concern are handled with confidence and confidentiality—

these are important factors in the church's proclamation of who and what it claims to represent.

I recall the experience of one church that had all the makings of a viable congregation. It was situated in a neighborhood rapidly changing from white to black and ideally located on a major thoroughfare, accessible to people from different parts of town. The pastor was a great preacher, and the church facility was more than adequate for potential growth. This congregation had all the makings of a mega church, but it had one drawback: It stagnated in the throes of various power struggles. The older members who had "paid their dues," were very suspicious of the new younger group and its "upstart" ideas. A climate of acrimony persisted, and accusations and recriminations tore the church apart. Members even began to bring weapons to church, threatening to kill each other. The church proclaimed one thing, but the interpersonal relationships among members said quite another.[3]

This church, which still contains great potential, was badly damaged by the raucously unchristian behavior of its members. The image of the church in the community was nearly irreparably tainted, and it is extremely difficult to recover from such a perception, once those negative messages have been conveyed to the larger community. Viewing new people as the "enemy" created a context for the disintegration and dissolution of the church. The festering of a few negative attitudes on the part of the congregation can spell the death of a church. Needless to say, the pastor's "wait and see" posture did not help matters.

What a church proclaims through the interpersonal relationships of its members has great influence on the church's reputation in the community from which it expects to draw new members. While recovering from such a poor image is not impossible, few people would relish belonging to a church were such seething cauldrons exist. Interpersonal relationships often do more to impact decisions about joining churches than the Sunday sermon, and often reveal more effectively what parishioners really believe about the faith they profess to practice. If these personal relationships are not hallowed on solid ground, the church has violated the first principle of prophetic evangelism.

Community Outreach and
Congregational Inreach

Prophetic proclamation for effective evangelism also has to do with how well a church *reaches out* to the community and *reaches in* to its present members and constituents.

A characteristic of the prophetic aspect of Jesus' ministry is that the people ran to tell others how the master had loved and healed them. The same principle applies to the prophetic church today. The famous axiom of T. S. Eliot is a useful phrase for prophetic evangelism: "The whole world is our hospital." The church therefore engages in the development of programs to meet the needs of both the outer and the inner community. The way the people in one realm are loved, ministered to, and nurtured will influence persons in the other arena.

The appeal of community outreach resides in the type of edifying programs offered to people outside the church. Being in touch with the needs of people in the larger community is essential to knowing what kinds of programs will appeal to them.

The lure of congregational inreach resides in the type of nurturing programs offered to people inside the church. Being in touch with the needs of people in the congregation is essential to knowing what nurturing is required by them.

If proclamation is the "show and tell" of the church's evangelical ministries, the programs offered to the outer and inner communities are the "proof of the pudding."

Perhaps outreach to the surrounding community does not require the developing of new programs at all. It may simply mean opening the church's doors so that community groups may meet regularly. Establishing the church as an open-door facility will truthfully proclaim the extent to which it will go to serve the community.

One pastor related an experience with a church that had developed a reputation in the community as being cold and uncongenial. Worship services were virtually empty on Sunday, and the church never opened its doors to people in the surrounding area. It was only after the church began to allow community groups to utilize meeting space that a noticeable change in worship attendance occurred. By simply opening its doors and creating a climate of outreach, it experienced growth.[4]

When more people began to attend Sunday services, the pastor went about evaluating their needs. An adolescent parenting group was started, along with an after-school sports program for youth. Within two years, these two programs alone netted approximately fifty new members. Such an increase was outstanding for a church that had lost an average of twenty members annually, over a ten-year period.

While community outreach can include the development of specific programs to meet the need of residents, it also can mean identifying the church as a place whose doors are always open to the people living in its midst.

Churches that don't grow, that die slow and sudden deaths, have usually closed their doors to the community in some form or another. In fact, in urban areas where crime and poverty are rampant and churches have declined in membership, doors have been shut out of fear. Many of the mainline denominations in predominantly black urban environments have not grown because they have failed to develop outreach programs which address the real needs of community residents.

Conversely, in churches which have managed to grow in these communities, one would invariably discover the presence of programs that speak to the ultimate needs and concerns of people in the community. The church that grows will open its doors, extend invitations to people to belong, and aggressively seek the larger community's support. Moreover, if people feel that the church is truly concerned about them, that it will leave no stone unturned and no avenue unexplored to help them live more spiritually productive lives, they will, by and large, support it.

One pastor told of his success in simply having town meetings at the church to resolve the problems of crime in the community. The response by community residents was overwhelming. In fact, the meetings were so successful that a task force was developed to take their concerns to the mayor and city council. Making the church a gathering place for community crises was enough to empower the people to take their concerns to the brokers of city government. What the church did through constructive action on behalf of the community *proclaimed* more about its relationship with Christ than words could ever convey. The proclamation that increases membership is manifested in action done on behalf of God's people. Again, people who were empowered by this movement subsequently joined this church because it reached out to them during a time of need.[5]

When the community needs a prophetic response from the church, the "ostrich approach" will not suffice. This method advocates looking the other way, or burying one's head in the sand, in regard to the critical concerns of both the outer community and the inner church. Prophetic proclamation means conveying the essence of religious conviction through transformative action, which leads to positive and constructive change in the lives of individuals and the larger community. Sincerely exemplifying such care and concern is an excellent tool for prophetic evangelism. You can prophetically increase growth in your church by establishing viable programs of community outreach and congregational inreach.

The key here is to develop a balance between these two entities. I personally know pastors who spend more time tending to the needs of the larger community than to those of their own congregation. Their churches suffer from the "absent pastor syndrome." When in need, members invariably call upon whoever is available, which in numerous cases is someone other than their pastor. Striking a balance between community and congregational involvement is important, and the prophetic church always demonstrates a concern for both.

The success of any evangelism program is based upon how effectively the church backs up its claims of love, truth, and justice. People want to belong to a church that implements the central tenets of faith and belief through positive action, which leads to personal and social transformation. Develop your evangelism program with an eye toward creating a program around community and congregational needs.

The Sunday Sermon

We usually think of the Sunday sermon as a form of proclamation or kerygma of the Word of God. The sermon announces the reality of God and reveals the stance of a particular pastor and congregation toward the meaning of faith and fellowship. It is a highly effective evangelism instrument, for it shows and tells people what a particular church believes and embodies; it discloses its principles of faith and provides a glimpse into the way that faith is practiced in real life terms.

If the Sunday sermon is inspiring, informative, challenging, and uplifting, people will be compelled to attend church. If the proclamation is uninspiring, unprovocative, and depressing, people as a rule will not attend. In addition to interpersonal relationships, the Sunday sermon is an important proclamatory component of the church's ministry.

In African American communities, good preaching has always been a benchmark of church growth. Those churches with outstanding preachers in their pulpits often have large congregations. That's why *what* is proclaimed is just as important as *how* it's proclaimed. If the preacher "doesn't say it," people generally won't be present to hear it.

We say that the preached word is an important element of evangelism because in the Protestant tradition the kerygma is an indispensable part of worship. Black people as a rule will attend a church where there's good preaching, but more important, it must be preaching that faithfully proclaims the tenets of a crucified, resurrected, and liberating Christ!

In an era when so many media are contending for the minds and hearts of hearers, it is critical that preaching retain its vitality and attraction as an art form. People today are video-oriented. They not only *listen* to the music, they *watch* it on TV. I remember my father recalling the times as a boy when his family gathered around the table to *watch* the radio. Today children *watch* the music. The audio and visual orientation of people today is much different than it was forty years ago. Preaching must compete in an age of multimedia influences. Therefore what is proclaimed is just as important as how it is proclaimed, if people are to be won to Christ. This often means utilizing a dramatic medium for the proclamation of God's Word.

In order to compete with other media in today's world, preaching must contain a persuasive element. It must be punctuated by verve, enthusiasm, and something evocative, if it is to capture the minds and imaginations of hearers.

The what and how of the preacher's proclamation tell much about the nature and spirit of a particular congregation, and most often will become an impetus for joining a church. If the proclamation is spiritually energizing, thought provoking, awe inspiring, people often decide to return to the church to hear the preacher again. If he or she is consistent in the preparation and delivery of sermons, never cheating the congregation but always giving them the best, those who return may choose to belong to the congregation. As one older preacher commented, "Anybody can preach at least one good sermon a year. To be consistently good is exceptional."

There are those who take the art and craft of preaching seriously and often do good work in preparing their proclamations. If only one person can walk away from a sermon remembering one positive idea, then the sermon was "good" and worth every ounce of sweat and tears that went into it. If one soul can be saved for Christ, one life lifted from the dregs of despair, one doubt transformed into certainty, then the proclamation is worth its weight in effort.

The biblical prophets again become a standard of emulation in prophetically increasing the growth of African American churches, for *what* they proclaimed in the name of God was just as central to the life of Israel as *how* they proclaimed it. The passion, conviction, investment, and vision of biblical prophecy is essential for the proclamation of God's word today. Cutting through the cynicism and disbelief of people today requires a herculean effort by pastors and churches in living out the truth claims of their proclamations.

We stated that a characteristic of prophetic evangelism is that it proclaims through word and action the Good News of Christ, that churches grow because what is proclaimed verbally is translated faithfully into the lives of the people of God. *Proclamation essentially means reclaiming the lives of God's people through consistent belief and action which calls for the actualization of faith through the positive transformation of individuals and communities.*

Proclaim Christ by living Christ! Proclaim truth by living truth! Proclaim the transformative and liberating power of God's love by living it! The leadership and followership of the church should be living out these precepts through their mission and ministry.

PROPAGATION/COMMUNICATION

Evangelism programs that speak to the needs of community and congregation are important, but the *marketing and propagating of those programs is also essential to church growth.* Pastors and churches often have outstanding ideas for winning people to Christ and increasing their membership. But the way these programs are marketed is critical to sustaining long-term growth.

We mentioned previously the value of verbal communication in spreading the Good News of the church's ministry. Traditionally, this works well in African American communities. Service professionals build their practices in the black community by word of mouth. If people have a good experience and are satisfied, they will recommend a professional to others. This is true also of the church.

While this approach in regard to churches works well in some situations, the value of advertising cannot be overestimated. Those churches with successful programs usually have developed sound marketing strategies. *Marketing for Congregations* provides good insights into the what and how of church advertising.[6]

We live in a world where people are continually bombarded by marketing and advertising strategies. The propagation of information about a particular product is indispensable for success in selling that product to society. The advertising budgets of major corporations contain billions of dollars, because executives understand the necessity of disseminating the word about their product.

Churches, in developing viable evangelism programs which make them strong, should consider the modes in which they propagate their "product." Unfortunately, many people today still have antiquated notions about the church and find the idea of developing church marketing strategies sacrilegious. The church should not adopt the "ways of the world" in spreading the gospel, objected one opponent of this idea.

But why not? Does not the church offer as one of its products a place of refuge and healing in our society? Is not the pastor in some instances a sales representative who attempts each Sunday to announce the benefits of living the Christian way of life? In fact, says one colleague, the pastor must be a brilliant sales representative, because he or she is trying to convince people to commit their lives to a product that has benefits they can't always see. Unlike conventional salespeople, who have a tangible product that a customer can materially experience, the preacher announces to the congregation a product—the gospel—which has value that is usually not measured or quantified. This is especially true in trying to persuade people to try it the first time.

People often must be convinced of the efficacy of buying into the gospel and organized religion, since they can't always see the positive results in the lives of others who presumably have bought into it. George Bernard Shaw once stated that Christianity would be a good thing, if anyone ever tried it.

And the preacher is not the only sales representative of Christianity. The laity have a far more wide-reaching market. All professed Christians are really salespersons for Christ. Whether the church chooses to market itself or not, it does so unintentionally through the lives of its members. Each time a member of a congregation interacts with other people, he or she markets the church.

Successful evangelism programs understand the value and necessity of developing good marketing strategies to reach specific populations. In what ways are your current programs being marketed to the larger community in order to build your church? Church growth today requires that programs, ministries, and the unique offerings of the church be propagated to wider audiences. Such marketing can take the form of regular mass mailings, radio and television advertisement, the persistent involvement of church members in significant community programs, or the advertising of specific church programs geared toward bringing new people into the flock. There are literally thousands of ways to market the church in order to successfully increase membership.

In my own experience at Hope United Methodist Church, which recently received a church-growth award for the fastest growing church in the Detroit Conference, we have employed everything from "Each One Reach One" Sundays to newspaper advertisements and neighborhood canvasses.[7]

The people of Hope are always conscious of the imperative for communicating a spirit of aliveness and concern for the people around them. Because of this enthusiasm, both contagion and curiosity are generated, so that people become interested in the programs and ministries of the church.

Many people have stated that during the course of conversation, even with strangers, they will invariably mention the church and extend an invitation to visit. This is a good evangelism strategy, and although these persons may not be consciously marketing the church in a business sense, their expression of excitement and love for the church is a form of advertisement. If ebullience and enthusiasm are sincerely conveyed, people will want to visit the church, if only out of curiosity. Most people want to belong to something exciting. They want to be a part of a winning team. Winning teams display winning attitudes, and this is a critical component in winning people to Christ.

Propagation of the church's ministry through the communication and advertisement of its programs is an effective prophetic evangelism tool. One might ask, How can such a tool be prophetic?

Communication and propagation of the mission and ministry of the church is prophetic in that it disseminates a message of God's transforming power and love to a larger audience. A prophetic imperative is not only to *"tell others of what you have seen and heard,"* but to *faithfully witness to them about the efficacy and profundity of the Word of God as it is revealed in their lives.* The prophetic imperative is to place those who have not seen and heard always within earshot and eyesight of God's Word as it is disclosed in the human context. The prophet never ceases telling others of what he has seen and heard, and never refrains from exhorting them to full consciousness of the same transforming experience.

Similarly, it is incumbent upon the prophetic church to witness, to go and tell others about what it has seen and heard, that they too might experience the benefits of spiritual and social transformation. The fire and fervor of God's Word is too good to keep to oneself. Each person must be told of its magnificent power and grace, so that lives, communities, and nations can be transformed in God's image.

Prophetic evangelism recognizes the need for communicating, propagating, and disseminating the marvelous work of the Lord through the church. It moves beyond the provincialism and sectarian isolationism of old church norms, and affirms the need to reach people through new media and mechanisms. The prophetic church is unafraid to chart new territory, to try new methods and deploy different strategies to reach the hearts and minds of God's people.

Many find difficulty in propagating the church—not because they think it a bad idea per se, but because they themselves often don't burn with passion for the church's ministry. Their lives are not on fire with the warmth of the Lord's work. They don't go and tell others, because they themselves don't feel the flame of Christ burning in their hearts!

Churches that grow prophetically through evangelism are churches that are on fire with God's Word. They believe in propagating and communicating to others the glorious work of God in their lives. They don't mind witnessing to the truth of God's Word, because they have been the grateful recipients of positive transformation. Understanding the value and importance of bringing others into the fold, they go all-out to witness to others, to bring them into the body of Christ.

Countless churches throughout the country have established magnificent programs to benefit the congregation and community, but a major obstacle is the inability to communicate information about those programs. In talking with numerous pastors, I have repeatedly discovered the presence of great creativity in developing viable ministries, but a failure to make people in the surrounding communities aware of those programs, so as to maximize the growth potential of their churches. Good programs can attract people, if they know that such programs exist!

I recall the great struggle we had at Hope Church in instituting our first neighborhood evangelism canvass. The evangelism committee developed a beautiful brochure depicting the church and its ministries. Painstaking work went into the preliminaries. A plan was developed to visit homes in the surrounding neighborhood, drop off packets, and engage in conversation with residents about the mission and ministry of Hope Church.

Many people felt good about developing the packet and dropping them off at the homes of community residents. However, when asked to witness to neighbors about the church, panic set in, and people began to have second thoughts about the project. Several of the committee members were terrified at the idea of talking to others about the church.

"We don't feel confident," said one member. Another thought that since they had never done anything like that before, it would be a difficult thing to do. Ironically, a creative list *of excuses for not witnessing was rendered by members of the evangelism committee,* the committee commissioned to go out and witness to others! But they were afraid to do so.

After considering the responses, we decided to have training sessions on being disciples and witnessing for Christ. I discovered through this experience that people were reluctant to "tell others" because they felt they had nothing for which to witness. Many were literally ashamed of the prospect of aggressively going out and sharing the ministry of Hope United Methodist Church. One woman even stated, "Methodists don't do those things. That's for Jehovah's Witnesses."

Prophetic evangelism believes in propagating the gospel of Christ and the ministry of the church through a variety of programs. If people are fearful of bringing others to Christ, training programs should be established to teach them the basics of discipleship. Education will help to dispel fear and instill the confidence necessary for sharing Christ with others. This may take months or years of appropriate training. Other programs of advertisement and marketing should be cultivated also, to give the church's ministry more visibility in the community.

Training for volunteers is essential, for they must have an understanding of human nature. They must be inviting but not pushy, aggressive without being offensive, patient, sensitive, and willing to be convicted for their convictions. In short, those who prophetically witness for Christ must have a sense of the overall mission and ministry of the church and an idea about how people can be persuaded to belong to the Body of Christ.

They also must have a grasp of how the mission and ministry of the church have transformed their lives and be capable of sharing its various aspects and nuances. The average person, when approached, will ask themselves, "How do I feel about this person and what he or she is saying? Will this church program be of benefit to me? If so, why? If not, why not?"

Those who prophetically proselytize for the church must have a clear understanding of how their lives have been transformed through Christ. They must have knowledge about the psychological, cultural, and spiritual context of the people to whom they witness. Thoroughly in touch with the *when, where, why, what, and how of their own spiritual journey,* they should reveal how the church has facilitated their positive spiritual transformation. Having the capability of telling others about our own experiences begins the process of helping others to envision themselves as worthy recipients of God's transforming grace.

In chapter 1, we stated that the four characteristics of biblical prophecy are *passion, conviction, investment,* and *vision.* In developing a prophetic evangelism program and training volunteers for mission, emphasis should be placed upon all four characteristics, but especially upon *conviction.*

Evangelists for the prophetic church must be tough-minded and tenderhearted. They must be prepared for opposition and rejection, but be so committed to their mission and goals that no impediments will thwart their efforts. Without conviction, they are repelled by rejection and deterred by opposition.

Equally important in the propagation process is sharing information about the various programs of the church and their benefit with those who will tell others. If the educational ministry of the church is doing exciting exploration into the African foundations of Christianity, find creative ways to share this information. If unusual programs exist for youth, adults, or seniors, tell people about them. The uniqueness and vitality of current church ministries should be shared with potential members. This is an important feature of prophetic evangelism because it discloses the central constructs so essential to faith-building within the beloved community.

In witnessing to others about the church's ministry, express *excitement, passion,* and *joy.* One of the great flaws that destroys enthusiasm for the Lord's work is the tepid manner in which we convey our message.

One pastor shared his experience in developing a coterie of willing and able evangelists. The volunteers went through tedious training and fulfilled all requirements to be disciples of Christ. One problem: They lacked the enthusiasm that wins people. They witnessed to others, but had no impact because of the absence of excitement and joy in their sharing.[8] By exuding joy in their witnessing, evangelists personify the reality of having been possessed fully and truthfully by that to which they are giving testimony.

Why would I attend your church, when your witnessing is about as exhilarating as peas in a pod? How will you convince others about the magnificent, glorious vision of the church when you talk as though it were some Poe-like tale from the crypt? Some people have more enthusiasm for a last-place team than they do for the church! Where's the excitement, the fervor, the zest and zeal for the Lord's work? This is what convinces and persuades people to visit your church!

The prophetic voice is always a passionate voice. It is filled with the intensity and reverberations of cosmic possibilities. It is punctuated by joy and jubilation, flanked by ecstasy, euphoria, and rhapsodizing grace. The intimacy and ultimacy of the prophetic proclamation is imbued with an exigency and urgency which transcends the prosaic, commonplace, and pedestrian.

Similarly, the prophetic church has a prophetic voice which speaks passionately and fervently across the bland banalities of modern life and cuts through the trite, insipid conventions which defuse it of its spark and spectacle.

Implicit in propagation and communication, then, is a message that blazes with the fury and fires of human possibilities yet unscorched by the seething embers of pessimism and despair. Those who would prophetically tell others the story of the church's mission and ministry must be immersed in the glow and warmth of the Body of Christ. Other people won't catch fire for the church unless we are on fire for the Lord!

Why should Christians let the world outdo them in showing enthusiasm for the things they love and enjoy? Vitality is contagious. If people can show excitement for the cars they drive, the homes they live in, the teams they support, why can't Christians show joy for Jesus? If anything kills a viable evangelism program, it is the lack of ardor by those called to witness to God's love and truth as revealed in their lives.

Joy should be made manifest in everything, from personal witnessing to the experience of worship. Black people, as a rule, don't tell people about a dead church. They won't invite people to a church if it lacks the spiritual propellants that drive and uplift the human spirit, that dispel depression, doubt, and despondency. People want a church that's alive and stimulating. They want to be with people who share the joy of living life through Christ. Martin Luther once observed that he had been around good boring Christians for so long that he longed for the company of an honest-to-God sinner!

PARTICIPATION

The prophet invites the people of God to reflect critically upon their life as shared through the covenant. She also invites full, unadulterated participation in the process of Kingdom-building for the Lord. Invitation must be followed by a call to actively participate in the Lord's service.

The key to successful prophetic evangelism lies in finding ways to invite and solicit participation from all the people in the life of the church. This means that programs must be developed for people of all ages and categories, to meet a variety of human needs.

Remove the Barriers

A great problem of mainline denominations in general, which has significantly contributed to a decline in membership, has been the impediments to participation in the life of the church. Because historically, membership in these denominations has been a means of conferring social status upon individuals, the churches themselves have developed strict requirements for participation. One generally could not be involved in the church activities without first becoming a member. For some, this was an incentive to join.

For others, it was a stumbling block. The famous statement by Woody Allen in the film *Annie Hall,* that "everyone wants to become a member of a club that won't accept him," illustrates a mentality manifested in the early days of some mainline denominations.[9] While strenuous requisites for membership and church participation may have been fashionable at one time, today it is perceived as a deterrent to church growth.

The "for members only" stance of some churches has precluded the possibilities for growth, since only the "initiated" can participate. Only those who look, act, and smell "like us" are encouraged to belong.

A pastor of a congregation in the Midwest complained that his church could never grow. Upon closer examination, he discovered one reason: It had always had a "for members only" ministry.[10] When visitors came to the church for worship, they were repelled by the cavalier, arrogant, purse-proud way they were received. They were never welcomed, never asked to participate in the life of the church. In essence, they were never "courted" or made to feel at home. Unless the church changed its stance from coldness toward strangers and visitors to active, open participation, it would never experience growth.

What current obstacles to church growth and participation exist in your church? Are there barriers such as inordinate membership requirements? Is there an unamiable disposition toward visitors, or a general climate of intolerance toward new ideas and progressive change? The elimination of encumbrances to participation is a first step toward membership growth.

Another example of membership barriers has to do with the presence of some people who serve on the governing boards of churches for long periods of time. Not that I personally have anything against long and fruitful leadership tenures, but some people overstay their leave and lose touch with the fundamental purpose of the church.

Some new people in the community who desired to join a certain congregation came upon the idea of establishing a scout troop at the church. It would keep their sons off the streets, give their children something constructive to do, and serve as a "gift" to the church's ministry.

The chairman of the board nixed the idea, since "the church does not have enough storage space and the troop's presence would create more wear and tear on the building." Other creative ministries designed to meet the needs of both parishioners and community were similarly rebuffed by this individual. The problem is that he lost sight of the church's basic purpose—to serve the people of God. He was more interested in preserving the edifice than meeting the needs of people. Many members left that church, and some prospective members refused membership because of the obstacles to participation personified by this one man.[11]

While each church has specific requirements about serving on special boards and agencies, and nonmembers cannot serve on governing committees, the overall ethos of involvement has much to do with the spirit of fellowship generated by the laity. While active participation may not mean sitting on a particular committee, it may mean immersing oneself in the camaraderie and fellowship of church life. Everyone in the church, visitors or members, should feel a desire to participate in some aspect of the church's life, be it choirs, Bible study, or other activities. No membership requirements are needed here for people to enjoy fellowship. Lyle Schaller rightfully differentiates between the membership and the fellowship circles of the church. The aim is to include all the people within the fellowship circle. That's where the action is, where a sense of belonging is created.

The prophetic church works hard to find ways to solicit participation in the life of the church. Through the experience of community with others—sharing life stories and collectively claiming the truths of the faith—personal and communal transformation can be realized within the context of the fellowship community.

In many cases, if people are not met with the smoke screen of membership prerequisites and are genuinely invited to become involved in various activities, formal membership will result. Before electing to enter a congregation, some people like to work in the church to determine how it feels, to better discern the spirit and attitude of those with whom they serve. If the church feels good, if a spirit of genuine love and caring is experienced by the person while serving, he or she may want to unite because of the sense of belonging garnered there. *Such persons should never feel, however, that participation in the church is predicated upon membership. An open invitation to participate is the gift of growing churches. All barriers to participation by nonmembers therefore should be summarily removed.*

Create a Context for Belonging

Encouraging participation in the life of the church simply means creating a context for belonging where all the people of God, both members and nonmembers, can sense the possibilities of human transformation and fulfillment. One of the greatest elements of prophetic evangelism is the creation of a climate, or atmosphere, where people feel that a sense of wholeness and wellness can be achieved. This feeling of well-being emanates from a sense of belonging which creates a desire to participate in the life of a particular church.

As a child growing up in the city, I recall always wanting to belong to those groups where things were really happening. The first characteristic of the groups to which I wanted to belong was that they were having fun and fellowship, which I, not being a member, was not having. Second, a joy that I couldn't experience as an individual was generated by the group. Third, the group was always goal-oriented and achievement-minded, so that some collective mission or project was part of its objective.

Whether it was the neighborhood baseball team, the Scouts, the youth fellowship of our church, or a confederacy of dedicated marble shooters, belonging to those groups could give me something that being alone could not.

The same is true of the prophetic church. In order to grow, it must create a sense of belonging, a desire on the part of others to participate in the life of the church. People should be so turned on by what they see, hear, and feel that they can't live without it. In order to create a context for belonging so that people will feel the need to participate in the life and ministry of the church, the following philosophy or theology must be espoused.

First, everyone is a child of God, and this includes female and male, young and old, rich and poor, black and white, employed and unemployed, the haves and the have nots. Every person in creation is worthy of the best that God has to offer. The church must incorporate this into the working paper of its organizational theology and evangelical outreach.

Second, no individual should feel estranged in the church, that he or she doesn't belong there, is unwelcome or unwanted. An ethos of acceptance for anyone and everyone should be genuinely established, even to the most and the least of these.

Third, the language of outreach, caring, and sensitivity should always be utilized by those in the church—language which facilitates spiritual awareness and promotes a sense of belonging for each person. If some haven't been to church for several Sundays, call on them. If you haven't seen them for weeks, don't judgmentally say upon seeing them, "Where were you, we haven't seen you!" Say instead, "Glad to see you! We missed you!"

Fourth, each person should feel needed and encouraged to offer his or her gifts, talents, and graces for the glory of God in the church. Whether it's folding envelopes, playing an instrument, or laying bricks, each person has been blessed with a talent that can be of use to the church. People must feel that whatever their gift, it can be utilized and appreciated within the context of the church's mission and ministry.

Fifth, never say no to people who desire to offer themselves in service to God. If at least three persons want to start some special ministry, give them some permission to innovate. Often, the offering of a service becomes an inroad to belonging and participating in the church.

While all five principles are important in creating a sense of belonging, the fifth is especially crucial. That is, creating a feeling of belonging can be manifested in the church's acceptance of visitors or in the way it receives people desiring to share their talents. It can also be created by the manner in which it receives new ideas from new people.

The point here is that people may choose to belong to a church in various ways. They may desire to share a talent or gift, or offer an idea that can enhance the church's overall ministry. The climate of belonging is created by the way the church allows people to come and get involved in its life and ministry.

Numerous pastors have shared frustration at the zero growth condition of their churches. Upon further examination, we have discovered that in many of those situations, the older members have not created an ethos of belonging for potential members. Further scrutiny also reveals a climate of intolerance for new ideas from new people, and a general stonewalling of the people who desire to share their gifts.

One pastor related that certain members of his church were up in arms about one woman who was folding the weekly bulletins for the church. While this gift may seem mundane and rudimentary, the truth is that the woman had a gift for doing such meticulous things. Some members of the board felt she should be a member before being allowed to participate in such activities. All people have at least one talent which they can execute better than others, and they should be given an opportunity to share that gift for the glory of God and the good of the church. It's their way of giving back to God something of value, and this makes for belonging, which leads to joyous participation.

Empower Women Leaders

There is an old adage that in the black church, women run everything. In many black churches, women do far outnumber men, but often they do not fill the traditional leadership roles. Seldom, if ever, will you find a female chairperson of the deacon board, or even a female deacon, for that matter.

The prophetic black church affirms a model of ministry which advocates the placement of women in key leadership roles. This may mean electing a woman chairperson of trustees, a role traditionally reserved for men. This step is highly innovative and will help to create belonging and participation for all.

In order to achieve this goal, the congregation should be educated about the necessity and importance of cultivating female leaders. The African American church still remains very male-dominated and highly paternalistic. While women have strong roles as the mothers, the movers and shakers of many congregations, they still largely have not been given the nontraditional leadership roles and respect due them from their male counterparts.

Sadly, many black churches struggle with the problem of *whether God can call a woman to preach*, never realizing their true potential because they still haggle over such basic propositions. The prophetic black church challenges and denounces the traditional reactionary assumptions that women cannot lead the people of God effectively and cannot be called by God to do so.[12]

A climate of acceptance of female leadership in nontraditional roles is highly needed to create an atmosphere of belonging and participation. It will also help grow the church. Women can function as chairpersons of finance, trustee, stewardship, and deacon boards. In fact, by encouraging such participation, a church will often experience quantum growth.

Create Programs for Male Empowerment

A perception that women run the black church truly exists. It may be, as stated earlier, that since more women *attend* church, this perception has developed credence.

The challenge for the prophetic church in creating a sense of belonging and participation is to find ways to solicit more male involvement in the life of the congregation. This often means developing programs that meet the needs of black men.

One program that has proven effective at many churches is the male support group. This group meets on Sunday mornings to discuss issues of critical importance to African American males, and also serves as a recruitment center for males in the larger community. Emphasis should be placed on nurturing and empowering African American men (rather than on denominational agenda or support of a national society), and should be an integral part of the church's outreach ministries.

The ideal church is one in which the leadership consists of male and female, young and old, with a context for mutually affirming and caring to benefit all. An environment is thus created in which all the people feel the importance of becoming involved in the nurturing process. Thus the church becomes stronger in its mission and ministry, and all who participate feel vitally connected with the larger vision and purpose for which the church is called.

Clear the Way for Youth

Youth programs are the mother's milk of prophetic evangelism and go a long way toward creating a climate for full participation of all people. If the church has as its mission a ministry for youth, then it has a good chance of growing fully and positively.

Too frequently, the church's attitude toward youth views the group as second-class citizens. This is a very destructive position for the church to take. Youth belongs not to the church of tomorrow, but to the church of today. In dying churches and in those experiencing no growth, you probably will find the conspicuous absence of meaningful, viable youth programs. If anything kills churches or stunts their growth, the dearth of programs for youth is usually the cause.

In order to create a climate of full participation and belonging, programs that speak to the needs of youth must be developed. One recurring problem in achieving this is that adults often feel they know what's best for youth and insist on developing the programs. A better approach is to solicit the participation of young people and allow them to shape the programs in accordance with their needs, with some adult assistance and supervision. The imperialistic, paternalistic, patronizing attitude of adults often prevents good youth programs from emerging in the church.

Reaching youths where they are in order to develop meaningful programs means understanding something about their world, the way they think and perceive life around them. It often means sitting where they sit and discerning life through their eyes, instead of through the mind-set of an adult.

A feeling of belonging must be extended to the youth. They are constantly evaluating themselves in relation to the adults around them. Adults must make concerted efforts to reach youth by speaking their language, knowing their music, and entering the "head set" of their world. This means listening and learning, allowing the youth to educate adults about their world.

This attitude goes far in helping to bridge the generation gap between youths and adults. By entering their world and utilizing the thought forms, expressions, and language of youth, adults are better able to get in touch with the way youth really thinks.

It would be helpful to include Youth Sunday each month in worship. Here the youth would lead the service in every capacity. The sermon would be specifically designed for them, which again removes barriers for full participation. It would be good for the church to have youth socials and other events which encourage fellowship, since much of their orientation is to be in community with their peers.

An effective tool of church growth is a relevant youth program. I have found that if youths are turned on by the church, they will often motivate their parents to attend, or at least to visit the church to see what it has to offer. If the programs truly speak to their needs, teenagers will tell their friends, parents, and associates, who may come out of curiosity, to see what the church is doing and what programs are provided.

In developing a youth ministry in her church, one pastor had to go to great lengths to convince an older congregation of the necessity for such a program. The general attitude of the people was that the young are irresponsible and irrepressible, and both were negatives for the church. Needless to say, the average age of members was fifty-five, and no programs for youth existed. That church is now faced with the inevitable question of who will guide its future, because it has alienated the younger people of the congregation. Whenever the church estranges itself from youth, it sets the stage for its own demise.

I don't mean to oversimplify, but if more churches realized the importance of establishing and perpetuating programs which train young people morally and spiritually, and cultivate and strengthen them for leadership in the future, the problems of homicide, drug abuse, and violence would be reduced. In fact, recent studies have revealed that the one factor which influences youth avoidance of these maladies is the church. The African American church has always been a bastion of leadership and nurture for its youth. The prophetic black church realizes and understands the necessity of removing barriers from youth participation, so they may be encouraged to realize their greatest potential as children of God and citizens of this world.

In developing a viable youth program, it is essential that only those individuals serious about reaching youth *on youth's terms* be enlisted. The nature and scope of those programs should include leadership training, the imparting of biblical and spiritual knowledge to help them make the right decisions when confronted with controversial and painful choices, and a social and recreational component to provide creative and constructive outlets. A strong youth-fellowship organization is a start in the right direction.

Some of the programs that work include Rites of Passage, Teen Weekends to address issues of human sexuality, Valentine socials, excursions to amusement parks, and encounter groups which address matters of personal concern.

Beyond the B.S. (Bureaucratic Syndrome)

What other impediments prevent the positive growth of your church's membership? Are these barriers attitudinal, organizational, operational, structural? That is, do they manifest themselves in a variety of forms, such as the attitude of seasoned members toward newcomers, or are they impediments in the church structures themselves? These issues are important in determining those areas that need critical attention.

The issue of structure is critical because some churches are so bureaucratic that they are actually dysfunctional. The problem of B.S., the Bureaucratic Syndrome in churches, prevents them from effectively utilizing existing structures and functioning at optimum capacity.

For example, my denomination has become so bureaucratic that the work of the church is often inundated in the mechanics of maintaining committee structures, rather than developing through them the viable ministries that serve the people of God. Church people literally live to serve the structures, not the people for whom those vehicles are ultimately meant to reach. Evangelism committees, instead of going out to evangelize neighborhoods and win people to Christ, are often caught in the spin cycle of bureaucratic tendinitis. They can't go out because they are too cloyed by the labyrinths and mechanics of church bureaucracy. In order to grow prophetically, churches should find ways to remove those bureaucratic barriers which prevent effective ministry and positive church growth.

Other barriers can be manifested in the non-winning attitude of congregations. Some churches have wallowed in the quandaries and vagaries of nongrowth for so long that they scarcely believe the church can grow at all. Perhaps this barrier is one of the most debilitating of all, because the people have essentially lost hope and faith in their own ability to build and grow something vital. They equally have lost sight of God's desire to transform their situation into something new and exciting. Once the people have lost hope and do not believe the church can succeed, the reality of growth becomes an uphill struggle. We must find ways to eliminate the defeatist attitude of congregations toward positive growth. Nothing kills the possibility of church growth in a particular congregation as much as its disabilities.

Economic Empowerment
Through Programs of Self-reliance

We stated earlier that for the church to grow, it should develop programs that meet the needs of parishioners as well as those of the larger community. Such programs can include job training and retooling; programs to enhance the economy of local communities, such as food and housing cooperatives; entrepreneurial programs for people who want to start their own businesses; and a multitude of other enterprises.

The programs offered need not be biblical or spiritual in a traditional sense, but should offer people positive opportunities to transform their existential situation, which does have profound spiritual implications. What can be more spiritual than helping people cultivate a means of feeding themselves through employment? By developing creative programs which speak to a variety of human needs, the church reestablishes itself as the spiritual center of the community it serves.

The church should envision itself as the investment center of human and material resources. If possible, it can engage in capital investments, such as the acquisition of real estate and other holdings that will empower and benefit the people of faith. If the larger society fails to develop inroads to personal empowerment, why can't the prophetic church take the lead in this area?

Programs for empowerment of the larger community create a

context for its participation in the life of the church. Accordingly, the life of the church need not be simply what occurs in Sunday worship or church-sponsored programs, but equally can be in non-traditional areas such as economic development and political enfranchisement. By opening itself to these broader concerns, the church makes itself available to a larger segment of the population by offering programs to meet a variety of needs. The more assorted the programs, the better the church's chances of growing prophetically.

CHECKLIST AND SUMMARY
OF PROPHETIC EVANGELISM PRINCIPLES

Proclamation Checklist

____A. Are the interpersonal relationships at your church healthy?

____B. Is the community outreach at least as strong as the inreach?

____C. Is the Sunday sermon evangelistic, full of Good News?

Propagation/Communication Checklist

____A. Have you established an entity in the church that is responsible for communicating the nature and purpose of church programs to a wider audience?

____B. Do you train a cadre of volunteers who specialize in communication and encourage them to disseminate the ministry of the church through multiple media?

____C. Do you consistently communicate existing and forthcoming programs to both churched and unchurched populations, on a basis that meets needs first and increases membership second?

____D. Do you market, disseminate, and communicate, as much as you can, the purpose of the church and its ministry?

Participation Checklist

____A. Are you removing existing membership barriers to participation by nonmembers?

____B. Are you creating a context for belonging, for every person, by utilizing the language of caring and sharing, and by encouraging people to utilize their talents for the glory of God?

____C. Are you creating a climate of acceptance and gratitude for women who serve in nontraditional leadership roles?

____D. Are you creating programs for the empowerment of black males?

____E. Are you clearing the way for youth involvement in all aspects of the church's life and ministry, by reaching young people where they are?

____F. Are you removing other harmful barriers to positive membership growth?

____G. Are you developing meaningful and viable economic programs which invoke the larger community's participation in the life of the church?

CHAPTER SEVEN

Let's Get It On!

The way to increase the growth of churches prophetically in African American communities is to . . .

. . . *celebrate* the mission and ministry of the church and African American culture through worship and other festive activities;

. . . *invite* people to participate in the celebration of life in Christ;

. . . *inform* people of the ways personal and social transformation can be realized through the actualization of human potential;

. . . *creatively confront* evil and the corresponding impediments which thwart human fulfillment and wholeness;

. . . *comfort* and *restore* those who have experienced estrangement, brokenness, and alienation;

. . . *investigate* all aspects of historical and contemporary reality, as a means of developing alternative consciousness;

. . . *interpret* the Word of God and contemporary reality to *evaluate innovative* and *constructive* modes when encouraging individual *empowerment* and *transformation*;

. . . *apply* the precepts of the faith and their liberating and transforming elements;

. . . *proclaim* through word and action the love, truth, and transforming power of God;

. . . *propagate* the Word faithfully and diligently;

. . . *participate* in the mission and ministry of the prophetic church, and precipitate involvement from others.

While for our purposes these principles have been broken down into three per work area, all twelve can be effectively applied in each program of the church's ministry. For example, in the chapter on prophetic worship, we cited three principles: *celebration, invitation,* and *information.* The worship service incorporates prophetic growth in worship attendance. However, these tenets need not be incorporated only in the area of worship. They can be equally implemented, with similar results, in the areas of education, evangelism, pastoral care, or other aspects of the church's programming. Celebrating, inviting, and informing are great incentives for attracting people to church.

Similarly, in the chapter on education, the three principles are *investigation, interpretation,* and *application.* These precepts also can be applied in other areas. Each area of ministry in the church can successfully incorporate all these principles. For example, in developing a program for seniors, an investigation of rationale and needs, by interpreting and applying the specific components of the program, will largely influence its impact and viability for the people it serves.

The primary goal of the prophetic black church is to call the people back to God and to instill in them those precepts that will lead to their spiritual and social transformation and subsequent liberation. The prophetic black church utilizes these twelve principles as a means of attracting new people into its fold and as a method of personal empowerment for positive transformation.

A basic premise of prophetic church growth is that people are in dire need of personal and social reconfiguration, but must fathom the *what* and *how* of this process. The African American church best captivates people for this purpose by embodying or establishing the twelve prophetic principles within the program areas of its various ministries. These twelve principles will help facilitate this process to both obtain and maintain interest and support, once people have decided to attend the church.

For example, the Rites of Passage program, the principle of innovation incorporated in a program ministry of the church, will induce people to bring their children to enroll in this program. Once completed, there must be other equally innovative projects to maintain the interest and loyalty of youth and parents. The prophetic church understands that the principle of innovation leads to personal empowerment and transformation of the people of God.

Because people are seeking such qualitative changes in their lives, they will go to a church where such opportunities are offered. If church programs embody the very principles of creative change that people are seeking, the church stands an excellent chance of gaining new members who are of an equally progressive character.

The central characteristics of the prophetic black church is the personal empowerment and spiritual and social transformation of the people of God. This requires the development of programs which increase spiritual, social, and political awareness, and compel people to envision themselves as both the recipients of change and the transformers of reality. The primary goal is thus the realization of human potential for the actualization of personal and community wholeness and vitality.

Equally significant is understanding the norms and values of African American culture, with its propensity for psychic, spiritual, and historical truth, together with the valuation of positive relationships and Spirit-centered reality, influence the practice of prophetic principles. For example, developing an educational program which encourages progressive investigation and inquiry is indispensable in exploring the African foundations of the Judeo-Christian heritage. The exploration and affirmation of truth in black culture demands the development of an educational ethos which encourages the relentless and untrammeled pursuit of relevant information.

Black people who are politically and spiritually progressive generally seek pertinent information about their history and culture, and the church should be a mainstay for the acquisition of such knowledge.

Both the biblical precedents of prophetic engagement and the central tenets of African American culture uniquely undergird and inform the implementation of prophetic principles for black church growth. Each of the precepts speaks to the issue of empowerment and transformation of individuals and communities. The prophetic motifs of *passion, conviction, investment,* and *vision*, while biblically based, constitute the requisites of prophetic engagement. African American culture provides the interpretive matrix by which black people apprehend and actualize the meaning of those principles of positive transformation culturally transmitted. Prophetic growth principles, as implemented in the African American church, provide a context for synthesizing both the biblical tenets and the central elements of African American culture into a practical framework.

Essentially, we have a confluence of principles from various traditions, welded into a manual which facilitates the prophetic growth of African American churches.

These principles are meant to be guidelines for developing growth programs through the prophetic tradition; they underscore positive transformation as an ultimate value and objective in the life of the church. Individuals who practice these principles will grow spiritually in Christ. Churches that practice them will grow prophetically in membership.

One central contention in this book has been that prophetic principles must be adopted if these churches are to dispel the racist and nebulous images they exhibit in African American communities. The image of opaqueness is a principle reason these churches haven't experienced more growth in black communities.

Accordingly, black pastors must not be afraid of being black, of affirming and celebrating biblical faith and African American religion, spirituality, and culture. They must not negate the rich and brilliant heritage of black people by apologizing to white or black people for what God has given them or by emulating uncritically the Eurocentric norms of religious behavior. They must equally challenge those intracultural and intraracial assumptions and beliefs that stifle the growth and development of African American people: discrimination against women who are fully gifted and capable of leading the people of God, and adoption of nonprogressive models of ministry which do not inspire the creative transformation of the African American condition. They must vouchsafe those traditions of value in African American culture by recapturing and revaluing the importance of jazz and the principles of innovation which help to create and shape our alternative consciousness.

Only by developing programs that speak to the issues of truth, healing, personal empowerment, and social and spiritual transformation, can the African American church capture the hearts, souls, minds, and imaginations of future generations of black people. Only by recovering those values and practices which affirm the primacy of women, men, and children, and celebrate the gifts and possibilities of both our individual and our collective being, can the church realize maximum potential for growth.

The prophetic black church also believes in the economic empowerment and redevelopment of African American communities and provides leadership in its cultivation. It affirms the political and spiritual enfranchisement of African American people for the realization of positive transformation in the home, community, society, and world. It accentuates the establishment of principles of self-reliance which compel churches and communities to discover and utilize their own potential and resources for change and growth.

The prophetic church embraces and actualizes the transformation and liberation of the people of God from every impediment and constraint that precludes the maximization of human potential. This means liberation from racism, sexism, ageism, and every other "ism" that stifles the progressive growth of human personality and potential.

The realization and actualization of human potential through the positive, progressive affirmation of personal and social transformation is therefore the hallmark of the prophetic black church. Freedom, justice, equality, economic empowerment, personal and communal reliance, political enfranchisement, spiritual wholeness and vitality are the principal objectives of the prophetic black church.

The task invariably is to call the people back to God; to tell them the Good News of a crucified, resurrected, and liberating Christ; to provide them with the spiritual and material resources which enhance the realization of their maximum human potential, a potential which, when realized and celebrated, will inevitably lead to the transformation of individual souls and the collective communities they inhabit.

The prophetic black church announces and personifies the

coming of the new heaven and the new earth, the Kingdom of human wholeness, vitality, and liberation. It exemplifies and embodies the love and truth so essential for positive growth and change. By developing these twelve principles, your church can grow in a powerful, positive, and progressive way, for "where there is no vision, the people perish."

You can prophetically increase growth in your church, *but if you fail to plan, you plan to fail.* An intentional, systematic plan is needed. Reliance on short-term gimmickry and other "state of the art" tricks for church growth seldom have long-term results. Study your context, dig in, and initiate the practice of prophetic principles. Don't be afraid of hard work, of struggling in the trenches until you achieve positive results. Time lines for success cannot be predicted, but numerous studies indicate that the five- to ten-year plans for growth are most feasible.

So celebrate, invite, inform, clarify, creatively confront, comfort and restore, investigate, interpret, innovate, evaluate, apply, proclaim, propagate, and participate in ways that will prophetically make your church grow!

Appendix

The Principles Simply Cited

1. Celebrate	life through Christ and the mission and ministry of the church.
Inspire	people to celebrate through worship.
Value	gifts, graces, presence, and input.
Consecrate	people for service.
Motivate	people to examine their lives and communities in ways that lead to positive transformation.
2. Invite	people to participate and belong in the fellowship and ministry of the church.
3. Inform	people of ways their lives can be transformed and enhanced through the church.
4. Clarify	needs, values, direction, and purpose.
5. Creatively Confront	evil or problem areas that can be found in the church's ministry.
6. Comfort	those suffering, in pain, broken, alienated.
Restore	them to life and wholeness.
7. Investigate/ Observe	facts and context of biblical and contemporary reality.
8. Interpret	ways to shed new light on role and impact of African culture on Christian developments.
Innovate	programs.
Evaluate	programs.

9. **Apply**   Christian principles and precepts, and teach others.

10. **Proclaim**   the Good News of Christ by developing programs that reach community and congregation.

11. **Propagate/ Communicate** programs of church in community.

12. **Participate**   in programs and encourage others to belong.

Bibliography

Adams, Arthur Merrihew. *Effective Leadership for Today's Church* (Philadelphia: Westminster Press, 1978).

Adams, James Luther. *The Prophethood of All Believers* (Boston: Beacon Press, 1986).

Barna, George. *Marketing the Church: What They Never Taught You About Church Growth* (Colorado Springs, Col.: NavPress, 1988).

_____. *User Friendly Churches* (Ventura, Calif.: G. L. Publications, 1991).

Ben-Jochannan, Yosef A. A. *African Origins of Major Western Religions* (Baltimore: Black Classic Press, 1991).

Blau, Peter. *Bureaucracy in Modern Society* (New York: Random House, 1956).

Brawley, James P. *Two Centuries of Methodist Concern: Bondage, Freedom, and Education of Black People* (New York: Vantage Press, 1974).

Bruggemann, Walter. *The Prophetic Imagination* (Philadelphia: Fortress Press, 1978).

Carothers, J. Edward. *The Paralysis of Mainstream Protestant Leadership* (Nashville: Abingdon Press, 1990).

Claerbaut, David. *Urban Ministry* (Grand Rapids: Zondervan, 1983).

Clements, R. E. *Isaiah and the Deliverance of Jerusalem* (Sheffield, England: JSOT Press, 1984).

Cone, James H., and Gayraud Wilmore. *Black Theology: A Documentary History 1966–1979* (New York: Orbis Books, 1979).

Crockett, Joseph V. *Teaching Scripture from an African-American Prespective* (Nashville: Discipleship Resources, 1990).

DeVinney, Richard. *The Wednesday Workout: Practical Techniques for Rehearsing the Church Choir* (Nashville: Abingdon Press, 1993).

Doran, Carol, and Thomas H. Troeger. *Trouble at the Table: Gathering the Tribes for Worship* (Nashville: Abingdon Press, 1992).

Dudley, Carl S. *Building Community Ministries* (Washington, D.C.: Alban Institute, 1992).

Dulles, Avery. *Models of the Church* (New York: Doubleday, 1974).

Easum, William. *How to Reach Baby Boomers* (Nashville: Abingdon Press, 1991).

Felder, Cain Hope, ed. *Stormy the Road We Trod* (Minneapolis: Fortress Press, 1991).

Fields, Rick. *The Code of the Warrior* (New York: HarperCollins, 1991).

Freire, Paulo. *Pedagogy of the Oppressed* (New York: Seabury Press, 1970).

_____. *The Politics of Education* (South Hadley, Mass.: Bergin & Garvey, 1985).

Galbraith, John Kenneth. *The Anatomy of Power* (Boston: Houghton Mifflin, 1983).

Geaney, Dennis J. *The Prophetic Parish* (Minneapolis: Winston Press, 1983).

Gottwald, Norman K. *The Tribes of Yahweh* (New York: Orbis Books, 1979).

Hacker, Andrew. *Two Nations: Black and White, Separate, Hostile, Unequal* (New York: Macmillan, 1991).

Hanson, Paul. *The People Called* (New York: Harper & Row, 1987).

Heidinger, James V. *United Methodist Renewal: What Will It Take?* (Wilmore, Ky.: Bristol Books, 1988).

Heschel, Abraham. *The Prophets* (New York: Harper & Row, 1962).

Hickman, Craig R. *Mind of a Manager, Soul of a Leader* (New York: Wiley & Sons, 1990).

Hodgson, Peter C. *Revisioning the Church* (Philadelphia: Fortress Press, 1988).

Holsinger, James W., Jr., and Evelyn Laycock. *Awaken the Giant* (Nashville: Abingdon Press, 1989).

Hunt, Earl G. *A Bishop Speaks His Mind* (Nashville: Abingdon Press, 1987).

Johnson, Douglas W., and Alan K. Waltz. *Facts and Possibilities: An Agenda for The United Methodist Church* (Nashville: Abingdon Press, 1987).

Kraeling, Emil G. *The Prophets* (New York: Rand McNally, 1969).

Lang, Bernhard. *Monotheism and the Prophetic Minority* (Sheffield, England: Almond Press, 1983).

Lasch, Christopher. *The Culture of Narcissism* (New York: Warner Books, 1979).

Lincoln, C. Eric. *Race, Religion, and the Continuing American Dilemma* (New York: Hill & Wang, 1984).

_____, and Laurence H. Mamiya. *The Black Church in the African American Experience* (Durham: Duke University Press, 1990).

Lindblom, J. *Prophecy in Ancient Israel* (Philadelphia: Fortress Press, 1962).

Matthew, Shailer. *Jesus on Social Institutions* (Philadelphia: Fortress Press, 1971).

McClain, William B. *Black People in the Methodist Church: Whither Thou Goest?* (Nashville: Abingdon Press, 1984).

McClemore, Clinton W. *Honest Christianity* (Philadelphia: Westminster Press, 1984).

Mitchell, Henry H. *Black Preaching: The Recovery of a Powerful Art* (Nashville: Abingdon Press, 1990).

_____. *Celebration and Experience in Preaching* (Nashville: Abingdon Press, 1990).

Mohney, Ralph W., and Nell W. Mohney. *Church of Vision* (Nashville: Discipleship Resources, 1990).

Neuhauser, Peg C. *Tribal Warfare in Organizations* (New York: Harper & Row, 1988).

Nichols, Roy C. *Doing the Gospel: Local Congregations in Ministry* (Nashville: Abingdon Press, 1990).

Niebuhr, H. Richard. *The Kingdom of God in America* (New York: Harper & Row, 1937).

_____. *The Purpose of the Church and Its Ministry* (New York: Harper & Row, 1956).

_____. *The Social Sources of Denominationalism* (New York: World Publishing, 1957).

Niebuhr, Reinhold. *Leaves of the Notebook of a Tamed Cynic* (New York: Meridian Books, 1957).

Orlinsky, Harry M. *Interpreting the Prophetic Tradition* (New York: Hebrew Union College Press, 1969).

Peck, M. Scott. *People of the Lie* (New York: Simon & Schuster, 1983).

Petersen, David L., ed. *Prophecy in Israel* (Philadelphia: Fortress Press, 1987).

Scott, Nathan. *Mirrors of Man in Existentialism* (Nashville: Abingdon Press, 1978).

Schaller, Lyle. *Activating the Passive Church* (Nashville: Abingdon Press, 1972).

_____. *The Change Agent* (Nashville: Abingdon Press, 1972).

_____. *Growing Plans: Strategies to Increase Your Membership* (Nashville: Abingdon Press, 1991).

Shawchuck, Norman, et al. *Marketing for Congregations* (Abingdon Press, 1992).

Shelp, Earl E., and Ronald H. Sunderland. *The Pastor as Prophet* (New York: Pilgrim Press, 1985).

Snyder, Howard A. *Liberating the Church* (Downers Grove, Ill.: Inter-Varsity Press, 1983).

Stallings, James O. *Telling the Story: Evangelism in Black Churches* (Valley Forge, Penna.: Judson Press, 1988).

Stewart, Carlyle Fielding. *God, Being, and Liberation: A Comparative Analysis of the Theologies and Ethics of James H. Cone and Howard Thurman* (Lanham, Md.: University Press of America, 1989).

Von Rad, Gerhard. *The Message of the Prophets* (New York: Harper & Row, 1962).

Walls, Jerry L. *The Problem of Pluralism: Recovering United Methodist Identity* (Wilmore, Ky.: Good News Books, 1986).

Ward, James M. *The Prophets* (Nashville: Abingdon Press, 1982).

Washington, Preston Robert. *God's Transforming Spirit: Black Church Renewal* (Valley Forge, Penna.: Judson Press, 1988).

Weber, Max. *On Charisma and Institution Building*, ed. S. N. Eisenstadt (Chicago: University of Chicago Press, 1968).

White, R. E. O. *The Indomitable Prophet: A Biographical Commentary on Jeremiah* (Grand Rapids: Eerdmans, 1992).

White, Woodie W. *Confessions of a Prairie Pilgrim* (Nashville: Abingdon Press, 1988).

Whitley, C. F. *The Prophetic Achievement* (London: A. R. Mowbray & Co., 1963).

Wiley, Ralph. *Why Black People Tend to Shout* (New York: Birch Lane Publishing, 1991).

Wilke, Richard B. *And Are We Yet Alive?* (Nashville: Abingdon Press, 1988).

_____. *Signs and Wonders: The Mighty Work of God in the Church* (Nashville: Abingdon Press, 1989).

Willetts, Sandra. *Upbeat Downbeat: Basic Conducting Patterns and Techniques* (Nashville: Abingdon Press).

Willimon, William H., and Robert L. Wilson. *Rekindling the Flame* (Nashville: Abingdon Press, 1987).

Wilmore, Gayraud. *Black Religion and Black Radicalism* (New York: Orbis Books, 1989).

Wilson, Robert R. *Prophecy and Society in Ancient Israel* (Philadelphia: Fortress Press, 1980).

Wimberly, Edward P., and Anne Streaty. *Liberation and Human Wholeness* (Nashville: Abingdon Press, 1986).

Wood, Forrest G. *The Arrogance of Faith* (New York: Alfred A. Knopf, 1990).

Woodward, Evelyn. *Poets, Prophets, and Pragmatists* (Notre Dame, Ind.: Ava Maria Press, 1987).

Notes

CHAPTER 1. FOUR TENETS OF PROPHETIC ENGAGEMENT

1. Walter Brueggemann, *The Prophetic Imagination* (Philadelphia: Fortress Press, 1978), p. 13.

2. Conversation with a Presbyterian pastor, July 1991.

3. Thomas Kochman, *Black and White Styles in Conflict* (Chicago: University of Chicago Press, 1981).

4. There are exceptions in both cases. This statement is not meant to be a generalization but is simply based upon observable patterns in both cultures. Numerous sections of the black middle class disdain anything resembling religious passion or emotionalism. Many blacks have joined predominantly white denominations to escape the specter of emotionalism that often characterizes the black church. Conversely, some whites are just as exuberant and fervent in expressions of cultural and religious behavior as blacks. Many white churches in various parts of the United States have worship services that resemble the more spirited worship styles of black churches. The norms of their culture make such expressions wholly acceptable and permissable. Each culture has exceptions which avoid prescriptive generalization.

5. Dietrich Bonhoeffer, *The Cost of Discipleship* (New York: Macmillan Publishing, 1975), p. 7.

6. Interview with a United Methodist pastor, May 16, 1990.

7. Conversation with a United Methodist pastor, July 17, 1991.

8. Chogyam Trungpa, *Shambhala: The Sacred Path of the Warrior* (New York: Bantam Books, 1986), pp. 8-9.

9. See M. Scott Peck, *People of the Lie* (New York: Simon & Schuster, 1983), p. 72. Peck defines evil as the failure to put ourselves on trial. Pastors must never exempt themselves from the same judgment they pronounce on God's people. The temptation is to exonerate oneself from that judgment simply because one is privileged to bring the message. The messenger is never exempted from the truth of the message.

10. Brueggemann, *Prophetic Imagination*, p. 13.

11. Informal conversation and interview with an AME pastor, June 12, 1991.

12. Edgar F. Magnin, *The Voice of Prophecy in This Satellite Age* (Cincinnati: Hebrew Union College Press), p. 110.

13. Conversation with a United Methodist pastor, September 10, 1991.

CHAPTER 2. PROPHETIC ATTRIBUTES OF MINISTRY

1. Wade W. Nobles, "African-American Family Life: An Instrument of Culture," *Black Families,* 2nd ed. (New York: Sage, 1988), p. 49.

2. Conversation with a resident of Southfield, Michigan, who shopped for a church home in the community for six months. Many people looking for a church require that the atmosphere and spirit of the church create a desire to belong. These are generally the more successful congregations.

3. See Monroe Fordham, *Major Themes in Northern Black Religious Thought 1800–1860* (New York: Exposition Press, 1975).

4. Conversation with pastor colleague on various improvisational aspects of African American culture.

5. This story is based on my own experience at Hope United Methodist Church in Southfield, Michigan. The struggle to improvise new curriculum for education is constant. A natural tension exists between the need to follow the *Discipline* to the letter or to interpret it according to the spirit. Perhaps both approaches work. However, knowledge of the context of ministry is, in many ways, more important than strict adherence to the text of denominational polity. The successful church utilizes organizational structures while maintaining the capacity to spontaneously develop programs and ministries that will meet the real needs of people.

6. Joseph L. White, *The Psychology of Blacks* (New Jersey: Prentice-Hall, 1984), p. 5.

7. Ibid., p. 28.

8. Wade Nobles, "Toward an Empirical and Theoretical Framework for Defining Black Families," *Journal of Marriage and Family* (November 1978), pp. 679-88.

CHAPTER 3. THREE PRINCIPLES OF PROPHETIC WORSHIP

1. Recollections of a United Methodist colleague. This data was garnered from an informal interview titled "Recollections" (1991). The pastor is serving a parish in Detroit.

2. Recollections of a Baptist colleague serving a parish in Detroit (1992).

3. Recollections of a Church of God in Christ pastor serving a parish in Chicago (1991).

4. This experience was related to me by a new member of Hope United Methodist Church in Southfield, Michigan (1992). The problem was that the pastor never varied his preaching themes. For five straight weeks, this person said he had not heard anything inspiring, challenging, or uplifting.

5. A statement made by a member of the Evangelism Committee of Hope United Methodist Church (1990).

CHAPTER 4. THREE PRINCIPLES OF PROPHETIC PASTORAL CARE

1. Informal discussion with a member of a United Methodist congregation in Detroit, Michigan (1992).

2. Henri Nouwen develops the metaphor of *The Wounded Healer* in his book of the same title. He discusses the phenomenon of the personal suffering of pastors, which serves as a basis for reaching out and ministering to others. The prophet's role is very similar. By calling attention to human suffering, the prophet helps create a context for the realization of healing and wholeness within the larger society.

3. "Conversations with Pastors: A Personal Memoir 1982-1992," an unpublished document of personal recollections over a ten-year period. Over the years, I have managed to record conversations with pastors about the struggles, trials, and victories of ministry. This conversation occurred May 28, 1989, in Detroit, Michigan.

NOTES TO PAGES 82–112

4. Ibid. (May 28, 1989).

5. Recollections of conversation with an Episcopalian pastor from Elizabeth, New Jersey (June 1987).

6. This story was related by a Baptist colleague living in Buffalo, New York (1991).

7. A United Methodist pastor in Detroit conveyed this story to me (1990).

8. Conversation related to me by a member of the Deacon Board of a local Baptist congregation in Detroit (1990).

9. "Recollections 1982–1992." This pastor serving a black United Methodist Church in Chicago related this story (1990).

10. "Recollections 1982–1992." The pastor who conveyed this incident served an Apostolic Church in Atlanta, Georgia. The story was told to me in 1986.

11. Ibid.

12. One of the criticisms leveled against the African American community is what appears to be over-reliance upon messianic models of leadership—so much so that if a catastrophe should befall a leader, the movement the person spearheaded loses momentum. Calls now are issued for more creative strategies for black leadership, including diverse styles and methodologies.

CHAPTER 5. THREE PRINCIPLES OF PROPHETIC EDUCATION

1. A great proliferation of information about African influence on world religions has emerged of late. See Josephus, *Halosis;* Robert Eisler, *The Messiah Jesus and John the Baptist* (London: Metheun & Co., 1931); Cain Hope Felder, *Stony the Road We Trod* (Minneapolis: Fortress Press, 1991); Jose F. Ben Jochannan, *African Origins of Major Western Religions* (Baltimore: Black Classic Press, 1991). Many more texts are exploring the African bases of the Old and New Testaments.

2. Experience of a black pastor in Los Angeles. Informal conversation, March 19, 1989.

3. G.W.F. Hegel developed this topology as part of his philosophy of history. See his *Phenomenology of the Spirit.*

4. Henry H. Mitchell, *Celebration and Experience in Preaching* (Nashville: Abingdon Press, 1990).

5. Avery Dulles, *Models of the Church* (New York: Doubleday, 1974).

6. This program was instituted at Hope United Methodist Church, Southfield, Michigan. There is nothing in the polity of The United Methodist Church that calls for the establishment of such a program. Its development is based upon the needs of African American youth in the Detroit metropolitan community. Similar programs can be developed in other churches, if the context is seriously studied in order to determine the real needs of African American people.

7. Jazz is *sacred* music. The same sacred energies, trials, tribulations, and struggles that engendered gospel and spiritual music have gone into the development of jazz. Numerous jazz musicians, from Coltrane to Albert Ayler, have viewed themselves as rotaries of global spirituality. It should be incorporated into the worship traditions of the African American church. Black people should not allow racist whites or reactionary blacks to determine what is valuable and sacred in the African American spiritual and religious traditions.

8. An experience of an African American female pastor serving a local United Methodist congregation. She confessed her lack of evaluation and preparation, but attributed this to a failure to pass the program at the board meeting.

9. These three principles are essential in conceptualizing and implementing prophetic programs for creative education. They are by no means exhaustive.

CHAPTER 6. THREE PRINCIPLES OF PROPHETIC EVANGELISM

1. One of the factors leading to a decline in the church's overall credibility among the masses is the "facing both ways" syndrome. Many people today are really confused—not about where the church stands on critical social issues, but where it stands in relation to practicing what it professes. The church proclaims to be open to people of all races. Yet Sunday morning church services are the most segregated hours in the American week. It proclaims to be interested in issues of personal and social justice, in opening its doors to the poor and dispossessed. Yet in many instances, if the poor and dispossessed would show up on the doorstep of many churches, they would be met with contempt.

2. These lines of division often create an "us versus them" mentality which leads to polarization of various groups. Church tribalism should be dispelled in every shape and form because it deters church growth. Prophetic proclamation seeks to transcend these divisions.

3. This experience was related by a colleague in ministry serving a Presbyterian congregation, 1990.

4. This experience was related by a pastor serving a United Methodist congregation, 1991.

5. This experience was conveyed by a United Church of Christ pastor, 1990.

6. Norman Shawchuck et al., *Marketing for Congregations* (Nashville: Abingdon Press, 1992); George Barna, *Marketing the Church: What They Never Taught You About Church Growth* (Colorado Springs: NavPress, 1988).

7. Neighborhood canvasses have always been a part of our evangelical emphasis. The church received a church-growth award based on the implementation of many of the principles delineated in this book.

8. Conversation with an Episcopalian pastor, 1991.

9. This statement is more or less paraphrased. The position of many mainline denominations has been their focus on belonging as a form of social status. In many instances, people belonged to these groups because of the social acceptability conferred. The idea that people will do anything to belong to a group that would not accept them due to social standing corroborates the stance of many mainline denominations in the early part of this century. H. Richard Niebuhr's *The Social Sources of Denominationalism* explores variant aspects of this phenomenon.

10. A United Methodist colleague coined this description of his church's attitude toward evangelical outreach.

11. Experience conveyed by a Baptist colleague and friend.

12. More black male pastors should join the struggles against sexism in the black church. Many of us have side-stepped this issue due to an overemphasis on traditional values and lack of prophetic conviction. This is an explosive issue that needs to be addressed if the church is to realize maximum growth. Both male and female pastors need to become sensitized to the other's issues.